Beaten Men and Violent Women
The Hidden Truth about
Domestic Violence in Australia.

B. Cameron Lee

DEDICATION

This book is dedicated to all men everywhere who are or have been victims of domestic violence at the hands of the women in their life.

ACKNOWLEDGMENTS

I would like to extend my thanks and appreciation to Dr. Augusto Zimmerman for his time and assistance in reviewing this book's content. Dr Zimmermann is Professor of Law at Sheridan College in Perth, and Professor of Law (Adjunct) at the University of Notre Dame Australia, Sydney campus. He is also President of the Western Australian Legal Theory Association, and a former Commissioner with the Law Reform Commission of Western Australia.

FORWARD: BEHIND THE DARK CURTAIN....

First of all I want to say that in no way do I want to make light of the impact of Domestic Violence on women in our society or condone violence against them but at least twenty five percent (25%) of the victims of domestic violence are men. One quarter of the total victims, and yet we hear nothing about them. No media coverage, not much mention in all the various Government publications and reports and certainly none in relation to meaningful assistance for these forgotten victims. Why not? In 2017 there was a reported 546,000+ men Australia wide who suffered violence at the hands of their female partners. (Government figures). It seems as if they are purposefully being overlooked. Hidden behind a dark curtain. Again, why?

So what are my qualifications to write an in depth book examining the facts surrounding the hidden domestic violence perpetrated by women on men? None really, except for the fact I suffered for eleven years at the hands of a woman predisposed to using her fists. I am not a 'victim', I'm a survivor and stronger for it. Why did I stay? For better or for worse is how it's supposed to go. Loyalty to ones mate. Do we cut and run at the first sight of trouble? In hindsight I should have. In my ignorance, I believed that patience and understanding might allow my partner to eventually realise there was no need for violence in our relationship. It didn't, and I discovered over time, when I sought assistance or made a cry for help, that there isn't any for men. In fact, life with a violent woman is a perilous tightrope to walk without being harmed or arrested as everyone knows, 'Only men commit domestic violence'. This is a fallacy. Some men don't make it through and choose suicide as a way out but this particular fact doesn't seem to be included in the official reasons for male suicides.

When I set out to write this book, my intention was to try and bring to light the plight of a relatively large number of men who suffer domestic violence at the hands of women but are ignored. It is a tale of injustice, discrimination and at times, derision. However, when I began to research the actual facts of the matter, I uncovered more and more societal influences which, singly or in combination, contribute to the continuing silence and the myths surrounding this ugly and little recognised facet of domestic violence. These very same influences actively interfere with an equal and fair outcome for male victims of domestic violence at the hands of their female partners. World wide studies indicate over forty five percent of non-provoked domestic violence, which includes physical abuse, is committed by women on men. This is not the small nor insignificant problem for the male victims of female violence it is portrayed to be.

These active societal influences all have some bearing on the silence surrounding domestic violence against men and the negative treatment they receive when seeking help. I felt the need to increase the scope of this book to include some of these influences. Although I lay no claim to being an anthropologist or a sociologist, I am capable of reading scientific papers and media articles relating to the problem and distilling some of the content into a manageable read. The idea is to try and create a basis for discussion and a possible resolution of the difficulties besetting this large number of men. It will be problematic, as to do so will require me to discuss, among other things, trends in modern feminism and its effects on today's society.

Unfortunately, to hold any discussion running counter to the populist, moralistic views surrounding a problem in today's society is not easy in the current political climate. I fully expect one or both of the following to occur to this offering. The first could be 'no-platforming'. This is a method by which most of the media, across its many outlets, actively refuses to give any coverage whatsoever to articles or news stories which challenge the current feminist, socialist viewpoints. The second method of avoiding any discussion regarding a topic in today's society is the application of moralistic labels to discredit the person or organisation trying to implement that discussion. Labels such as 'sexist', 'misogynistic' or 'racist' are enough to derail even the best intentioned work if enough virtue signalers get behind the negative labels and drown out any possibility of a reply or factual debate. Once a ruckus ensues, the media is more than happy to pursue the labeling rather than the issue itself and to negatively report on the situation rather than look into the root cause. I have recently heard this tactic expounded as, "It's more important to be morally right than factually correct."

So, here is a peek behind the dark curtain, where women inflict violence upon men, sometimes in horrific ways.

OVERVIEW

Rather than dive straight into a breakdown of many of the causes I perceive are involved in men being sidelined when it comes to domestic violence assistance, I will start with this overview of the current situation before going on to dissect the major points in greater detail.

Society is changing. Too rapidly for some, not fast enough for others. The Western values on which society is based, those same values which created the affluent world in which a lot of people now live and the democratic political systems which govern them, are being moved sideways in favour of some world wide Marxist aspiration to socialise the planet, while homogenising and moralizing its populations. It is Orwellian in nature, casting off a tried and true model for society, which is still capable of yet further fine tuning, to trumpet a new order which claims fairness for all yet vociferously shouts down and drowns out any and all opposing viewpoints. To quote Bella d'Abrera, Director of the Foundations of Western Civilisation Program at the Institute of Public Affairs in her 2018 article, 'What Version of Western Civilization are Universities Offering Students?'

"....every subject (in the study of Western Civilisation in Australia) is approached through the lens of identity politics, where class, race and gender is the primary focus. These left-wing leitmotifs have replaced the essential core subjects which explain the political, intellectual, social and material basis of the history of Western civilization. The concepts that should be transmitted to university students, such as *respect for the individual, equality of men and women under the law, the abolition of slavery, freedom of speech and religious toleration* are simply not part of the narrative and are not being taught." (Italics are mine)

In some respects, this societal change and the rate at which it is progressing has resulted in a marked superficiality with regard to considered thought concerning many of the issues being raised by their proponents. It appears there is a generalised shallowness in understanding the depth and breadth of some of the problems being faced by many in today's society, due most likely to a fair slice of the population now using smart devices to access the opinions of others and add their own uninformed, simplistic viewpoints to the general pool of moralistic outpourings. The epitome of this is the Fake News phenomenon.

This generalised lack of any real in-depth information has had a very real negative impact on the quality of present day interpersonal relations and the ways in which people interact with the society around them. Flick left, flick right. Not long ago, on a Facebook video posting by a reporter, I was astounded to hear a ranting young woman yell, with great seriousness. "It's more important to be morally right than factually correct."

Morals can be and are, a very liquid phenomenon in this day and age.

With this more instant moralistic and populist approach to formulating opinions, various groups in society and especially politicians, continually pour out more and more small, selective bites of generalised information to target a demographic. Portions of this information are selectively seized on by the media, which is now perceived by many as left leaning and a means of formulating public opinion. The information is then manipulated to serve its needs, often sacrificing truth and reality along the way. An example would be the nearly two year outpourings from many news organisations in the USA regarding President Trump's collusion with Russia, subsequently shown to be untrue. This socialistic viewpoint seems to have crept into nearly every facet of our society. Not so hard to believe when one considers that the Marxist socialistic viewpoint has been promulgated through Bachelor of Arts and Law degrees at universities since the nineteen seventies and even earlier. Nearly all people in positions of authority today, not only the Government and civil service but also lawyers, judges, media personnel and of course, university lecturers teaching their Marxist take on Western History, have qualifications from these various institutions. I am not saying that all were infected with this Marxist viewpoint but some have been. The effects are far reaching and insidious, sending tendrils into every aspect of society.

Politicians need votes and seem to swim like fish in the current of public opinion, seeking a position of secure popularity. As women make up around fifty percent of the voting public, so it is necessary for male politicians to be seen to be doing 'the right thing' for women. And not only politicians. This 'virtue signaling' has crept across most areas of society and every opportunity is taken to get out and 'protest' about moral issues and to be seen doing so, even co-opting young children to leave school for a day of protesting. After suggesting that protest effort would be better utilised being put into positive action to remedy the problem itself rather than just make noise, a respected, older, female media personality was recently branded 'racist' by a much younger, female millennial protester who didn't agree with that person's opinion.

Women themselves, especially those in positions

which have access to the media, have been championing the moral rights of women across all areas of society. This media outpouring eventually devolves to social media and as women are great communicators of emotion and feelings, ideas are taken up in an instant without a thought being given as to what they actually mean or the future outcomes of such actions. A tribe forms, based on ideas. Most of these almost instantaneous outpourings seem to decry men or the actions of men in general. Notice that this tarring with the moralistic brush is generally applied to all men, whether or not there are any facts involved. Facts don't fit in memes and often get in the way of a good movement. Hence, 'Only men commit domestic violence', is an oft repeated, erroneous statement which has taken root in society. Although any misogyny is instantly and loudly decried, this misandry seems to be acceptable to the moralisers.

Any form of opposition to these ideas, ideas such as 'All men are rapists' or 'all men are violent', is immediately shouted down by application of labels such as; *sexist, misogynist, racist, Nazi* or whatever vile label is applied to drown out any form of factual discussion about a topic. The trouble is, in the world of social media these labels themselves seem to stick and the mainstream media picks up on this, painting its own picture in favour of the name callers while giving very little airspace to any opposing views. Often careers and characters are quickly destroyed by this baseless gang attack while 'no platforming' effectively removes any form of self defence.

There are many grievances in society requiring considered discussion but it is not my intention to air them here as this book is about men who suffer domestic violence at the hands of their wives or partners and who are given no aid or assistance when it is desperately needed.

There are historical similarities to that which is occurring today, the Inquisition for instance. The Catholic Church once decided to hunt down 'heretics' and did so with a vengeance. It totally destroying the Cathars in the South of France with the First Crusade, a genocide. Once the finger was pointed and the word 'heretic' pronounced, the Inquisitors ground into gear. People were viciously tortured into admitting they were heretics then put to death for being one. After they had recanted of course. Anyone could point the finger and accuse someone of being a heretic. Needless to say, thousands upon thousands of innocent people, accused of heresy, witchcraft, vampirism or lycanthropy were murdered by the Catholic Church throughout Europe. There is a similarity in the later case of 'witchcraft' in North America. The Puritans of Salem in the USA are a good example. A young girl, after weeks of aberrant behavior, accused a neighboring woman of being a witch and negatively affecting her. It went on from there, with other people pointing out their own inconvenient neighbours and folk they didn't like until around two hundred people were accused of practicing witchcraft and twenty were executed. Later the colony admitted it was a mistake. Sound familiar? There are many parallels between these historical events and some of the media trials today. Many a professional career has been ruined by baseless accusation and finger pointing. It is well known that the taint of social disapproval sticks, even to the innocent.

It appears men are often being reviled as 'rapists' or 'wife bashers' and are generally considered by both the Government and the media as being the instigators and perpetrators of all domestic violence. This misandry is referred to as Gendered Crime, a convenient label. This is not the case though. In fact, world wide research shows that nearly fifty percent of unprovoked domestic violence is perpetrated by women on men. In Australia that figure is accepted to be around thirty five percent. It could be more. As there is need for presentation of the truth of the matter, I have chosen to write about the problem. Portions of this book will reveal the actual, true scope of the problem, quoting various peer reviewed, published studies from both Australia and overseas. I have chosen to include the titles within the body of the text as many readers don't bother consulting an appendix. Any interested reader can look up the actual facts to check the veracity of the quoted text. Further chapters will contain some discussion on history, societal influences, Government Publications by various bodies, factual research conducted in Australia and overseas, observations on the problems besetting male victims of domestic violence and some anecdotal stories.

What I find interesting is that even while the women's blows are raining down, the man is still being blamed for 'making her do it'. There are some horrendous tales of injuries sustained by men at the hands of women, including decapitation and dismemberment but they rarely, if ever, are reported on by the mainstream media and in a lot of cases there are no prosecutions of these women for their crimes. Some of these stories and the reasons for women escaping prosecution will be dealt with later on.

THE TRUTH

So, how does one begin to try and explain the current situation in society where there is so much attention being given to domestic violence perpetrated against women but virtually no attention when it concerns, at the least, over twenty five percent (25%) of Australian men who suffer domestic violence at the hands of women?

We need to go back quite a long way to start to explain some of the discrimination which is happening against men who suffer from domestic violence at the hands of women. The human race, in developmental terms, has only lately come to civilisation. Prior to around ten thousand years ago we were hunters and gatherers and lived in small bands or tribes. Accommodation was usually shared and everyone would have been aware of what everyone else was doing. Men hunted. Focusing on prey and its pursuit had evolved them to be single minded and strong. Women generally did the gathering and looked after the children, although there were exceptions in some societies. In their book, 'Why Men Don't Listen and Women Can't Read Maps,' by Allen and Barbara Pease, the reader is taken on a voyage of discovery to learn how much men and women actually differ in reality. The authors use the results of MRI scanning of active male and female brains to point out how men and women respond differently to the same mental stimuli. There have been many more experiments of this nature carried out since their book was first published and what those experiments show is that men and women *are* different, not just physically but also in how their brains work. Even the basic wiring is different.

Taken in the context of the hunter gatherer society, these differences have evolved so each sex has become somewhat more specialised for its role in that society. Although modern man no longer lives a hunter gathering existence, the sexes are still different, although their distinct roles are gradually disappearing. Evolution is constantly occurring and despite the influence of epigenetics its not always rapid enough to adapt us to new roles in an ever evolving society. This is not conjecture, the scientific evidence is abundant concerning how male and female brains function in a different fashion. They are anatomically hardwired differently before we are even born.

Once so-called civilisation came into being after the advent of agriculture allowed large numbers of people to live together in one place, rules had to be fashioned to avoid or resolve conflict. These rules are still evolving and becoming more complex and detailed all the time. A lot of Western society has evolved from the Judeo-Christian religions, the so-called children of Abraham which, incidentally, is also the root of Islam. In times gone by a wife would vow to 'love, honour and obey' her husband. This is an historical observation and does not necessarily reflect my personal feelings on the matter. However, in those times there was a need for a marriage to be a supportive arrangement and divorce was not an easy option. The roles of the sexes were well defined and mostly, men went out to work to support their families. My great grandfather for instance, worked twelve hours a day, six days a week for fifty weeks every year. On Sundays he was expected to go to church. His wife, my great grandmother, ran the home, looked after the house and the children and took good care of her husband so he could keep supporting the family unit. They lived until their mid eighties, still married.

The Bible, Torah and Quran and many other religious books, nearly all contain passages regarding disciplining wives. It seemed the patriarchal system of the time did not like opposition. Most of these passages, if not all, are contained in the Old Testament and are used to reinforce the idea of a Patriarchal Dominance Theory which is no longer of much relevance. Once upon a time, when religion was a big driver of society, a faithful and supportive wife was perceived as an important and valuable asset. Among the majority of Muslims, world wide, there is still a belief that a wife should obey her husband in all things and women need to be kept in line - by force if necessary. This forms part of the Muslim faith and is enshrined in Shariah Law. However, in modern Western society there is now no real place for such a religious anachronism, although it has tended to persevere in various socioeconomic groups and throughout various countries around the world.

The First World War started the transformation to a more egalitarian society while the Second World War really opened the door wide to the changes which have fundamentally altered the society in which most Western people live today. While a lot of men went off to fight and die, women moved into the workforce and occupied many positions throughout industry formerly held by men. Many stayed in those positions. This was the start of women becoming a larger part of the workforce. Eventually the Women's Lib movement gathered momentum to help bring about equality between men and women. In the mad rush forward for the perceived rewards of 'equality', a lot of people seem to have forgotten that 'equal to' does not necessarily mean 'the same as'. As an example: $5 + 3 = 4 \times 2$. Even the most rudimentary inspection of this equation would reveal that the figures on either side of the equal sign are not the same yet they are still 'equal'. Similarly it is possible for women to be equal in status to men in our society, without being the same as them, a point often overlooked by many.

As more and more research is conducted on both males and females of the species, the more it is revealed that the sexes are actually quite different and posses various innate strengths and weaknesses, both physical and mental. In reality, we are complimentary to each other and in realising that fact we should all work together to achieve common goals. However, this is not the case at present. There is a lot for us to learn regarding our similarities and differences, if there was enough interest in doing so. The information is out there but cannot be conveyed in just a few short memes on social media.

Before I discuss the women's movement and how woman interact with each other and with society, I need to address one of the most profound underlying issues of the present day, the push to replace Western style democracy with a Marxist socialism. This drive appears to be progressing on a world wide basis.

Western Democracy and its decline.

In the past, tribes, city states and countries were ruled by an aristocracy. This was either from a descended line of kings, a religious figure or a family with great wealth. Rarely were these representatives elected. In England, many years ago, the Barons and Nobles made King John sign the Magna Carta. They collectively imposed their will on the King. Mostly because individually, they had a lot of soldiers to fight with. Later, during the sixteen hundreds in England, Oliver Cromwell established Parliament, a voice for the people. Over the next three hundred years Parliament went through a number of transitions until the House of Commons became an institution one was elected to by popular vote. The Bills and Laws that the House of Commons produced still had to be approved and passed by the House of Lords, who occupied their seats by inheritance or being created a Lord by the English ruler. This is the people and Royalty working together. This model of democracy spread across the planet with the rise of the British Empire and has been adopted by very many societies in one form or another. Nearly all of them have some form of Lower and Upper House in their Parliament or Assembly, as having two houses virtually ensures some form of check on chicanery. Over time, this political system has been proved to work. Not perfectly but better than most other political systems. It has delivered a continually rising standard of living, individual wealth and freedom to its citizens and a welfare safety net for the less fortunate. My standard of living when I was very young would be considered abject poverty now but it was how people lived then with what they had. The Western Democratic system works so well that many countries which use it have become the targets of economic refugees, some of them from socialist countries, all eager to share the benefits of its lifestyle.

Detractors of Western Democracy, who are trying to float a socialist agenda, point to inequalities inherent in the system as a negative. There are inequalities but they are not so much inequalities of opportunity but more inequalities of result. Everyone gets a more or less equal start, give or take public school versus private school and similar observations but cream will rise to the top and for those who apply themselves, there is reward. This is equality of opportunity. In other words, we all get a chance at the start line to run our race. Some cannot be bothered to apply themselves though and give up.

Inequality of result is the situation where someone who has applied themselves and done well is castigated for having more than someone who didn't bother to try. There are calls for higher taxes and more equal distribution of wealth, so those who didn't make it have exactly the same rewards as those who did. On a personal level, why would I go to University for five years, graduate, then work eighty plus hours a week to see my money taxed and handed over to someone who prefers to sit around, doing nothing and complaining bitterly about their lot in life. Some of these people are professional 'victims'. Reread Aesop's fable about the ants and the grasshopper. Yes, we need our grasshoppers to fiddle for us, just not so many of them.

People who create wealth in a society, by bringing money into it from elsewhere, are actually enriching society as a whole and should be rewarded for their efforts. This is one of the tenets of Western Civilization, personal reward for personal effort. The fact that the Welfare System is in place for those less fortunate or those unable or unwilling to work is yet another benefit of Western Civilisation which has culminated in what we all have today.

Socialism doesn't work and is a means of controlling the population, especially if a central agency, such as the Government, is distributing the wealth. A brief look at Cuba or Venezuela, which should be a rich country, as examples of failed socialism illustrate the breadth and depth of corruption and poverty permeating such a society. I have been to Venezuela and seen firsthand the vast gulf between rich and poor. Although this inequality is obvious, even to those wearing blinkers, still the ideal of socialism is being promulgated by people who are indoctrinated by the social media idea of 'morals' but do no research. It is the promise of 'equality' which is constantly being promoted by its proponents which is espoused, an equality which does not exist.

The idea is not new. In an article in the Australian newspaper on 30th January 2019, Kristian Jenkins addresses the political indoctrination in schools. He quotes Antonio Gramsci, an Italian Marxist and communist politician, who early last century said that, "in the new order, socialism will triumph by first capturing the culture via infiltration of schools, universities, churches and the media by transforming the consciousness of society." Jenkins then went on to discuss the falls in literacy and numeracy and questions why Victorian and Western Australian schools are teaching radical gender and sexuality programs such as Safe Schools while so many children leave school barely literate.

What has this to do with Domestic Violence against men? Plenty. The Ramsay Centre is trying to establish a Chair for the study of Western Civilization. It is prepared to hand out a lot of money to do so but would like to make sure that the course taught is actually about Western Civilization and the grant is not subverted to another purpose. A number of major universities, who teach all sorts of courses, some funded by Middle Eastern money, have all refused to teach a course on Western Civilisation after some lecturers objected on the grounds that oversight by a Ramsay Committee member affected their academic freedom. These lecturers just happen to also espouse the socialistic viewpoint.

This viewpoint is a socialist utopia of equality, moralistic ideals, individual freedom and rights. To quote from Bella d'Abrera in 'What Version of Western Civilization are Universities Offering Students'.

"......the subjects they teach, and the extremely limited range of fields in which they specialise, are almost entirely confined to themes which fit Marx's model. As such, every subject is approached through the lens of identity politics, where class, race and gender is the primary focus. These left-wing leitmotifs have replaced the essential core subjects which explain the political, intellectual, social and material basis of the history of Western civilization. The concepts that should be transmitted to university students, such as respect for the individual, equality of men and women under the law, the abolition of slavery, freedom of speech and religious toleration are simply not part of the narrative and are not being taught."

The words which stand out in the socialist model are *identity politics, class, race and gender.* We will come back to them shortly.

A side effect of this socialist infiltration of society is Political Correctness, Being Offended and Being Discriminated against, all of which are designed to inhibit any reasonable responses or factual discussion. Following are three quotes from a tongue in cheek article by Daisy Cousens in The Spectator, Australia on the 29th October 2016 addressed to Leftist Millennial.

"….you've got political correctness all wrong. It's not about stopping people from being racist, or sexist, or homo/trans/ace/anything-else-phobic. That's called 'not being a jerk'. Political correctness is the inhibiting of *necessary* moral and practical judgment based on fear of defying popular opinion. It prevents us from addressing issues that are important, but uncomfortable."

"…..political correctness is sticking your head in the sand and allowing other people to suffer immeasurably because you don't want to be called nasty names like 'bigot'. Call me crazy, but isn't such selfishness contrary to the doctrine of compassion you keep ramming down right-wing throats?"

"….after years of arguing with you, Leftist Millennials, I've realised that when you assert everyone is entitled to an opinion, you mean only those that coincide with yours."

It's possible to see, in light of the above, how society is changing. This change is reflected in everything we do and say and, in the case of abused men, has placed them in an invidious position. To actually mention the problem of men being attacked by violent women opposes the current popular and widely held view of the Patriarchal Dominance Theory, an outdated idea from the past which sells the belief that men are responsible for all domestic violence. This is the height of misandry. To argue against it is to invite the wrath of outraged women and to be drowned in a slew of derogatory labels, all designed to avoid any logical and factual discussion of the problem. Many men, ordinary everyday husbands, partners and friends who have weathered the wrath of an outraged women, tend to keep quiet about the subject rather than speak out, mainly to keep the peace. Just think, you could lose over half of your Facebook friends overnight for voicing your own opinion or be bullied and trolled by those women who make themselves feel better and look good to their friends by their *virtue signalling*. Just like the fictional Kath and Kim – Look at me!

Modern Women and Modern Feminism.

The Women's Movement is not new. Women are very good at supporting other women and have done so for millennia. Look at the camaraderie shared in more primitive societies when gathering food or pounding clothes with rocks down by the river. As previously stated, women are different from men and their brains are wired in a different manner. In women, emotions permeate through a lot of decision making unlike the more single minded approach to problems exhibited by men. According to Alan and Barbara Pease in their book 'Why Men Don't Listen and Women Can't Read Maps', MRI scans of women and men handling the same emotional problem presented to them shows a linear fashion of brain activity for men as they think through the problem step by step but in woman, their emotions are linked to many areas of the brain at the same time, allowing for a more integrated approach. This has many advantages for the woman but doesn't readily allow for making a decision unburdened by emotion.

In modern society, the first real success of the Women's Movement was through the Suffragettes who managed, by a show of togetherness and the sometime use of force, to obtain the right for women to vote. After this they threw off the shackles of an archaic dress code and after the First World War entered the roaring twenties. It was not quite so much fun for the poor of the day but generally life was on the up until the Great Depression.

As previously mentioned, the Second World War resulted in a lot more freedoms for women as they took up jobs in many sectors of society which were previously only men's territory. Their contribution to the war effort was considerable and invaluable. When the swinging sixties hit and the pill became available, women took control of their destiny and Women's Lib took off. Unfortunately, many women decided they wanted to be 'equal' to men and set out to prove they could be. As previously explained, equal does not mean the 'same as' but that seemed to be the goal. Chivalry died slowly as many women resented the small displays of manners and kindness men showed them. Sometimes they even became aggressive about it which tended to result in these mannerisms gradually disappearing from society.

The internet was the next big step for women and they took to social media like ducks to water. Popularity was a prize and 'friends' and 'followers' became important. Once the internet was available on mobile phones, those phones went everywhere and are constantly being viewed. This interconnectivity essentially became the global 'village network' allowing women everywhere to connect and discuss and comment about anything. Tribes with 'like' ideas are formed across societal, cultural and geographic boundaries. 'Experts' on every subject under the sun raise their heads to give an opinion. Qualifications don't seem that important, especially when you can have thousands of followers, all participating in what you are offering. The language seems to have changed to accommodate texting and one can observe women and men sitting, looking at their phones, thumbs going ten to the dozen. It's so addictive that often their interaction with the actual, real world is much reduced in favour of their phone screens.

One problem with the need to be accepted in a group, even one so extended as to cover the world, is that having a very different opinion to your 'friends' can make you stand out like a rock in a stream and may result in mass condemnation and 'unfriending'. It's politically safer to go with the flow. One thinks of a flock of starlings, weaving and swirling through the internet as they choose the next direction to go in. 'Unfriending' is really in the same bag as bullying. A differing opinion is easily just ignored but casting someone out of a group and trolling them because of it is a definite statement. Cyber bullying is a way of keeping people in line or showing discontent with someone who has a different opinion to your own. Sharing the same opinion of what is 'right' and 'wrong' with everyone else is a form of *virtue signaling.* In effect you are showing that you are right behind your group's opinions or ideas. This has now become a global phenomenon and some internet users with massive amounts of followers are now capable of changing women's opinions and perceptions virtually overnight.

An example of this *virtue signaling* is the #Me Too movement, started by well known figures in the entertainment industry banding together and virtue signaling about sexual predation by males. Some older French women, like Catherine Deneuve, a film actress, thought all the fuss about how men interacted with women would reduce the incidence of sexual interplay (flirtation) between men and women to a rote pantomime. She added her signature to an open letter written about it which was backed by ninety nine other prominent Frenchwomen. Social media loudly and roundly condemned the letter in a Stalinesque fashion. Germaine Greer, one of modern feminism's originators and early protagonists of it has referred to #MeToo as ballyhoo. Ms Greer appeared to call the women accusing Harvey Weinstein of rape, sexual assault and harassment "career rapees" who used their #MeToo revelations to keep themselves in the public eye. She went on to lambast them for not coming forward sooner and went on to say, "It's pointless now bringing up this stuff, when for most of it no action can be taken. Why wait twenty years?"

This #MeToo phenomenon resulting from claims made against Harvey Weinstein reminds me of an anecdotal story said to come from a dinner party attended by Oscar Wilde. He was sat beside a rich, upper class woman and during the course of the dinner he turned to her and said, "Would you make love to me for fifty thousand pounds?" She replied that she'd have to think about it. Later, he turned to her and asked if she would make love to him for two pounds. "What do you think I am?" she responded. His reply was. "We've already discovered that Madam, now we are haggling over the price." With this story in mind, if a starlet is offered a part in a movie which would earn her money and fame, in exchange for sexual favours, what does the acceptance of the offer say of her moral fortitude? In my opinion, a truly moral individual would go back to her waitressing job. To then complain, twenty years and a lot of money and movie parts later that she was taken advantage of, rings slightly hollow.

Shock, horror, outrage! How dare someone say such a horrible thing about these poor 'victims'. Rather than discuss the issue however, the followers of the #MeToo phenomenon cannot allow any opposing view. As is often seen in memes, "We believe in free speech – as long as it agrees with our viewpoint." This is the culture of the present. Almost puritanical in its approach to men and a free and frank discussion regarding issues. It has resulted in some interesting advice being given to men in the business sector regarding care in not being alone during the mentoring of young women by male businessmen or not staying on the same floor of a hotel when travelling with female staff. They are also advised to avoid being in any situations where the man is left alone with a female staff member.

The internet has enabled Carl Jung's 'Collective Unconscious' to become conscious. Coupled with the ongoing demise of Western Democracy and the rise of the new Socialism, there is now less meaningful discussion than ever before. As previously mentioned, many men, politicians, media personalities and others in the public eye now have to be very careful of what they say and are perceived to do, as any little thing can be used against them and their lives and careers destroyed in an instant. Witness the proven unsubstantiated claims regarding a teenage drunken groping thirty years previously made by Christine Blasey Ford against a Supreme Court nominee in America. The media milked it. The public was outraged! Not against the fact it was a cheap, bare-faced political stunt but for the 'poor woman' making the claims. Incidentally, it is unknown what happened to the huge sums of money, reputed to be over $750,000 collected in two 'go fund me' accounts set up for her. The Democrats paid her legal fees.

In the current political climate, some art, this includes pictures, movies, books etc. is gradually disappearing from public view as its subject matter is considered to be 'unsuitable'. To whom? By who? What about all the people who make up the majority of the population who have been untroubled by these things for the last hundred years. Who tells who what is acceptable? That is the crunch. These groups of virtue signaling, self aggrandised people are setting a social agenda which suits their brand of moral intervention and that of their followers. This agenda may not suit the majority of the population but the majority has no platform to speak from and so the imposed ideological censorship continues.

This, I believe, is at the root of where the fairness regarding Domestic Violence has been corrupted. The message one repeatedly hears is; Only Men are Responsible for Domestic Violence. This is pure misandry and is the message which has been sold to everyone, including the Government of Australia, even in the face of large amounts of scientific evidence to the contrary. It is yet another example of The Emperor's New Clothes.

The next chapter will deal with that evidence.

ACTUAL EVIDENCE

It is not my intention to delve deeply into the science of the sexes to prove how different men and women are, this book is about domestic violence and how society is being sold a lie on what it is and how it manifests itself. The book is also about the inequality of assistance being offered to male victims of domestic violence compared to female victims. Also in the scope of this book is a brief comment on discrimination, as many people don't realise the Government is the biggest discriminator of its own citizens. The way the laws are set up, the Government can 'legally' discriminate in all areas it has legislated to do so, neatly circumventing the Discrimination Act.

First of all, I wish to comment on the 'fact' that all domestic violence is perpetrated by men. It isn't. For reasons listed in the previous chapter, it has become fashionable for all areas of society to take a moralistic attitude and parrot the lie which has been foisted upon us, in part by the Patriarchal Dominance Theory, a tool used by feminists to rally against men in general. This belief that all domestic violence is perpetrated by men seems to be upheld by some members of the police force. The same police force which is routinely called out to domestic violence incidents. Rather than reiterate some of the information eloquently laid out by Dr. Augosto Zimmermann in his paper, Women Can Be as Violent as Men, I have chosen to reproduce it here in full with the author's permission, complete with references, as it encapsulates the problems faced by men suffering domestic violence at the hands of women in Western Society.

Dr Augusto Zimmermann is Professor of Law at Sheridan College in Perth, and Professor of Law (Adjunct) at the University of Notre Dame Australia, Sydney campus. He is also President of the Western Australian Legal Theory Association, and a former Commissioner with the Law Reform Commission of Western Australia.

.

Women Can Be as Violent as Men

Augusto Zimmermann

Published 24th September 2018

Violence by women against men receives little attention, yet nearly four decades of research reveals they are also targets of physical abuse. Why the silence? Because the activists' ultimate goal is to tar all men, not just the relatively few perpetrators, as a collective and universally guilty group

You may have heard of a Perth-based family counsellor who was forced to resign from Relationships Australia WA (RAWA) after posting on his private Facebook page an article social commentator Bettina Arndt wrote a few years ago for the *Weekend Australian*.[1] The article summarised the latest official statistics and research on domestic violence, providing evidence that most domestic violence is two-way, involving women as well as men.[2] This was regarded as a breach of policy, because, on its own website, RAWA says its domestic violence policy "is historically framed by a feminist analysis of gendered power relations" which, contrary to the international evidence, denies women's role in domestic violence.[3]

By endorsing a feminist policy that is so morally bankrupt (and punishing a well-respected counsellor for refusing to do so)[4], this government-funded institution displays a disturbing lack of compassion for the wellbeing of all the male victims of domestic violence. RAWA's policy is based on a discredited approach that perpetuates the false assumption that domestic violence is always perpetrated by men against women. And yet, data keeps mounting which indicate that domestic violence may be perpetrated by both men and women against their partners. A decade ago an official letter by the Harvard Medical School declared that "the problem is often more complicated, and may involve both women and men as perpetrators". Based on the findings of an analysis of more than 11,000 American men and women aged eighteen to twenty-eight, the letter concluded:

When the violence is one-sided ... women were the perpetrators about 70% of the time. Men were more likely to be injured in reciprocally violent relationships (25%) than were women when the violence was one-sided (20%). That means both men and women agreed that men were not more responsible than women for intimate partner violence. The findings cannot be explained by men's being ashamed to admit hitting women, because women agreed with men on this point.[5]

The Harvard Medical School's letter was based on a seminal work published in the *American Journal of Public Health* in 2007. Written by four experts in the field (Daniel J. Whitaker, Tadesses Laileyesus, Monica Swahn and Linda S. Saltman), it seeks to examine the prevalence of reciprocal (that is, two-way) and non-reciprocal domestic violence, and to determine whether reciprocity is related to violence and injury.[6] After analysing the data, which contained information about domestic violence reported by 11,370 respondents on 18,761 heterosexual relationships, the following conclusions were reached:

• A woman's perpetration of domestic violence is the strongest predictor of her being a victim of partner violence;[7]

• Among relationships with non-reciprocal violence, women were reported to be the perpetrator in a majority of cases; [8]

• Women reported greater perpetration of violence than men did (34.8 per cent against 11.4 per cent, respectively).[9]

One explanation for these significant findings is that men are simply less willing than women to report hitting their partner. "This explanation cannot account for the data, however, as both men and women reported a larger proportion on nonreciprocal violence perpetrated by women than by men."[10] In fact, the authors explain that women's greater perpetration of violence was reported by both women (female perpetrators = 24.8 per cent, male perpetrators = 19.2 per cent) and by men (female perpetrators = 16.4 per cent, male perpetrators = 11.2 per cent).[11] Based on the information available, the authors concluded:

Our findings that half of relationships with violence could be characterised as reciprocally violent are consistent with prior studies. We are surprised to find, however, that among relationships with nonreciprocal violence, women were the perpetrators in a majority of cases, regardless of participant gender. One possible explanation for this, assuming that men and women are equally likely to initiate physical violence, is that men, who are typically larger and stronger, are less likely to retaliate if struck first by their partner. Thus, some men may be following the norm that "men shouldn't hit women" when struck first by their partner.[12]

Unfortunately, violence by women against men is a phenomenon that has received little attention in the media and in government. Yet for nearly four decades the best research reveals that men are also frequently the targets of violence by female partners. Since the 1980s more than 200 academic studies have demonstrated that, despite the common assertion, most partner violence is mutual, and that a woman's perpetration of violence is the strongest predictor of her being a victim of partner violence.[13] Across several countries the best research available shows that the percentage of men who are physically assaulted by their female partners tends to be remarkably similar to the percentage of women physically assaulted by their male partners.[14] However, those who deny the empirical evidence often resort to unacceptable tactics, which includes "concealing those results, selective citation of research, stating conclusions that are the opposite of the data in the results section and intimidating researchers who produced results showing gender symmetry".[15] One of the leading researchers in the field, Dr Murray A. Straus, has received numerous death threats, as have his co-researchers, Dr Richard Gelles and Dr Suzanne Steinmetz, with the latter the subject of a vicious campaign to deny her academic tenure and rescind her grant funding.[16]

Australian media and government reports often frame domestic violence merely as "violence against women". This generates a totally false assumption that males are always the aggressors; that men are the only ones capable of harming their partners. For instance, you may recall the federal campaign on television two years ago. These ads were part of a $30 million campaign designed "to help break the cycle of violence against women and their children".[17] It seemed to suggest that all of the perpetrators of domestic violence are Caucasian males.[18] The Prime Minister even assured us that his domestic violence campaign was all about creating "a new culture of respect for women".[19] Malcolm Turnbull, a self-described feminist, concomitantly launched a $100 million "women's safety package", apparently because violence against women in the home is on the rise. In his words: "All disrespect for women does not end up with violence against women, but let's be clear, all violence against women begins with disrespecting women."[20]

More recently we have seen further calls to action from Mr Turnbull to "change the hearts of men", and from the Opposition leader, Bill Shorten, to "change the attitudes of men", as if there were some kind of unspoken bond between these politicians and the men who commit violence against women. "Not all disrespect of women ends up in violence against women but that's where all violence against women begins ... but what we must do ... is ensure that we change the hearts and minds of men to respect women", Turnbull says.[21] Shorten says, "All this violence is ultimately preventable and ... we need to change the attitudes of men."[22] While these political leaders see no problem in offending the Australian people by assuming that violence against women is an "accepted part" of our society, Claire Lehmann, the editor of *Quillette*, reminds them that in our society "crimes against women are stigmatised and punished harshly. Sexual offenders generally are given lengthy prison sentences and are secluded from other prisoners precisely because the crime is so reviled—even in prison".[23] And yet, in the distorted world of identity politics:

> *individuality is subsumed into the collective. When one man holds power, he doesn't do so on behalf of himself, he does so on behalf of the male collective. Likewise, when one man commits a murder, collectivists will portray it as being done in the service of all men. This regressive worldview has no qualms about ascribing collective guilt to entire groups of people. But ascribing collective guilt strikes at the very heart of our understanding of justice and liberty.[24]*

Clearly these two federal leaders believe their statements on this matter will have popular support, particularly from women voters. But judging from the letters received by journalist and sexologist Bettina Arndt, who wrote an article in the *Australian* in 2016 about research showing the prominent role women played in violence in the home, there are many in our community, including many women, who are extremely uncomfortable with gender politics. She received an avalanche of supportive letters, not only from professionals working with families at risk from violent mothers, but also from many women who had grown up in such homes, or had witnessed their brothers, fathers and male friends experiencing violence at the hands of a woman. As she points out, "many women commented how surprised they were that Turnbull made such an offensive, one-sided policy announcement".[25]

Women can be as abusive as men

Professor Linda Mills, the Ellen Goldberg Professor at New York University, is the principal investigator of studies funded by the National Science Foundation and National Institute of Justice, which focus on treatment programs for domestic violence offenders. Her studies in the field are published by *Harvard Law Review*, *Journal of Experimental Criminology* and *Cornell Law Review*. As she points out:

Years of research, which mainstream feminism has glossed over or ignored, shows that when it comes to intimate abuse, women are far from powerless and seldom, if ever, just victims. Women are not merely passive prisoners of violent intimate dynamics. Like men, women are frequently aggressive in intimate settings and therefore may be more accurately referred to as "women in abusive relationships" (a term I prefer to the more common usages "battered women," "victim," or "survivor") ... The studies show not only that women stay in abusive relationships but also that they are intimately engaged in and part of the dynamic of abuse. As the studies of lesbian violence demonstrate, women are capable of being as violent as men in intimate relationships. And women can be physically violent as well as emotionally abusive. That violence comes out in their intimate relationships both as resistance and as aggression. We need to put aside our preconceptions of gender socialization and roles.[26]

Erin Pizzey, the woman who set up the first refuge for battered women in 1971, knew from the very beginning that women can be as violent as men in domestic relations. She herself was raised by a violent mother who used to beat her with an ironing cord until the blood ran down her legs. Pizzey strove in vain for her mother's love. She was left badly damaged by her regular beatings and verbal abuse. She was called "lazy, useless and ugly" by her mother, who often called her father "an oaf and an idiot" and depicted his mother as a "prostitute" and his father as a "common Irish drunk".[27] In Pizzey's own experience, women are just as capable of domestic abuse in both the physical and emotional sense. When she opened a refuge for battered women in England, sixty-two of the first 100 women to come through the door had been as abusive as the men they had left.[28] So when the feminists started demonising fathers in the early 1970s, her own memories were a sober reminder that:

Women and men are both capable of extraordinary cruelty ... We must stop demonising men and start healing the rift that feminism has created between men and women. This insidious and manipulative philosophy that women are always victims and men always oppressors can only continue this unspeakable cycle of violence. And it's our children who will suffer.[29]

Erin Pizzey is part of a growing number of brave experts and scholars trying to set the record straight.[30] As early as the 1980s academic researchers such as Dr Murray A. Straus, a professor of sociology at the University of New Hampshire, have developed research demonstrating that women are just as likely as men to report physical and emotional abuse of a spouse. These findings have been confirmed by more than 200 studies of intimate violence and they are summed up in Dr Straus's article "Thirty Years of Denying the Evidence on Gender Symmetry in Partner Violence".[31] This article indicates that most partner violence is mutual and self-defence explains only a small percentage of partner violence by either men or women.[32] Rather than self-defence, "the most usual motivations for violence by women, like the motivations of men, are coercion, anger, and punishing misbehaviour by their partner".[33] As Dr Straus points out:

Pearson (1997) reports that 90% of the women she studied assaulted their partner because they were furious, jealous, or frustrated and not because they tried to defend themselves. These motives are parallel to the motivations of male perpetrators. Research on homicides by women shows similar results. For example, Jurik and Gregware (1989) studied 24 women-perpetrated homicides and found that 60% had a previous criminal record, 60% had initiated use of physical force, and 21% of the homicides were in response to "prior abuse" or "threat of

abuse/death." A larger study by Felson and Messner (1998),
drawing upon 2,058 partner homicide cases, determined that 46%
of the women perpetrators had previously been abused, but less
than 10% had acted in self-defense.[34]

In the United States, estimates from national family violence surveys show that within a given year, at least 12 per cent of men are the targets of some sort of physical aggression from their female partners, with 4 per cent (or over 2.5 million) of these men suffering severe violence.[35] In another pioneering study in America, the clinical sample found "the eruption of conjugal violence occurs with equal frequency among both husbands and wives".[36] This study included several statements by women who often abuse their husbands. "I probably had no reason to get angry with him … but it was such a bore. I was trying to wake him up, you know. He was such a rotten lover anyway. So I'd yell at him and hit him to stir him up," said one woman.[37]

In Britain, female domestic violence against men is clearly on the rise. Data from Home Office statistical bulletins and the British Crime Survey reveal that men made up about 40 per cent of domestic violence victims each year.[38] Seventeen men were killed by their female partners in England in 2012 alone. [39] Furthermore, British men are twice as likely as women to keep their abuse undisclosed, primarily because of cultural barriers and a legal system that does not protect them.

"They feel emasculated. Their pride is undermined and they are reluctant to see themselves as victims," says Mark Brooks, the chairman of Mankind, a charity for male victims of domestic violence.[40] Even so, "every year our helpline is seeing at least a 25 per cent increase in the number of men seeking help".[41]

Of course, the percentage of reported male victims would be considerably higher were it not for the sexist biases of the system. As noted by a journalist in the *Guardian*, men assaulted by their wives and girlfriends are often completely ignored by police. They are often treated as "second-class victims" and many police forces and councils do not take them seriously. "Male victims are almost invisible to the authorities such as the police, who rarely can be prevailed upon to take the man's side," says John Mays of Parity, an organisation that advocates equal treatment of domestic violence victims, both male and female, and their children. Their plight is largely overlooked by the media, in official reports and in government policy, for example in the provision of refuge places—7500 for females in England and Wales but only sixty for men.[42]

The official UK figures notoriously underestimate the true number of male victims of domestic violence. This is so because men in Britain are extremely reluctant to disclose that they have been abused by women. Culturally it is still enormously difficult for men to bring these incidents to the attention of the British authorities. It certainly does not fit the false narrative that women are supposed to be always weak and never the perpetrators of domestic violence. But it is patently clear that both men and women can be victims of such violence, and that "men feel under immense pressure to keep up the pretence that everything is OK", said Alex Neil, a Scottish politician who was Cabinet Secretary for Health and Wellbeing at the Scottish Parliament between 2012 and 2014.[43]

As for Australia, the Australian Bureau of Statistics Personal Safety Survey reveals that proportions of non-physical abuse (for example, emotional abuse) against men have risen dramatically over the last decade, with 33 per cent of all people who reported violence by a domestic partner being male.[44] And yet, one of the tactics used by domestic violence campaigners is to highlight only men's violence and leave out any statistics relating to women. There is constant pressure to present domestic violence as a "male problem", and place all the blame for such violence on men as a collective group. As a result, and based on a theory that addresses the problem essentially as a male problem, male victims are often met with disbelief, even suspicion, when they seek protection from a violent partner.

-

Consequences of the denial of female domestic violence

Domestic violence against male partners is grossly under-reported. Frequently men do not conceptualise the physical violence they sustain from their female partners as a crime. Indeed, studies in the field indicate that men are reluctant to report assaults by women, "even when severe injuries result".[45] This reluctance is prevalent among male domestic partners, perhaps because they are expected to be physically dominant. Admitting to sustaining violence from a female partner may be viewed as "emasculating".[46] Further, when domestic violence is conceptualised as a crime in these surveys, women are significantly less likely to report their own use of violence. Some research reveals that women fail to report as much as 75 per cent of their own use of violence.[47] According to Professor Donald G. Dutton and Dr Katherine R. White:

One reason that intimate partner violence toward men is underestimated is that men are less likely to view [domestic violence] as a crime or to report it to police. Men have been asked in survey if they had been assaulted and if so, had they reported it to police. In a 1985 survey, less than 1% of men who had been assaulted by their wife had called police (Stets & Straus, 1992). In that same survey men assaulted by their wife were less likely to hit back than were wives assaulted by their husband. Men were also far less likely to call a friend or relative for help (only 2%) ... Historically, men who were victims of assault by their wives were made into objects of social derision. ... Men are socialised to bury problems under a private veil, including being the object of abuse from female partners ... Either the women are bragging or the men are in denial, or both.[48]

This under-reporting of female domestic violence is partly explained also by the fact that men who sustain this form of violence are unlikely to seek help for these issues out of a reasonable fear "they will be ridiculed and experience shame and embarrassment".[49] If they do overcome internal psychological barriers, they still face unfair external institutional barriers in seeking help from social services and the criminal justice system. For instance, male help seekers often report that when they call the police during an incident in which their female partners have been violent, the police sometimes "fail to respond or take a report".[50] Indeed, male victims of domestic violence encounter greater animosity when contacting the police. This can be contrasted to the "positive and supportive attitude" of the police to women who accuse their husbands of violence. According to Sotirios Sarantakos, an adjunct professor in the School of Humanities and Social Sciences at Charles Sturt University:

Most interesting is the finding regarding the practice of women running to the police after hitting the husband, although they hit him without a reason. Even threatening to go to the police was often taken very seriously by the husbands—not without reason. The positive and supportive attitude of the police and authorities to women's position was reported to have encouraged many wives to take advantage of this and to become even more aggressive at home. Even when they had severely assaulted the husband, their statement that they had been assaulted and abused by him at that time or previously was sufficient for the police to treat them as innocent victims[51]

Men are far more likely to be arrested for domestic violence than their female partners, even when other factors including previous arrests are taken into account. A study in the United States reveals that men face harsher legal ramifications post-arrest: 85 per cent of violent men were arrested and prosecuted by the police, compared to only 53.5 per cent of violent women.[52] Some of these men are actually innocent and report "being ridiculed by the police or being incorrectly arrested and convicted as the violent perpetrator, even when there is no evidence of injury to the female partner".[53]

This might explain why so many men who sustain violence are deeply reluctant to report on their partners. Compared to abused women, there are few social programs or non-profit organisations providing useful assistance to men who are the victims of domestic violence.[54] Instead, male victims often experience external barriers when contacting these social services. When they locate the few resources that are specifically designed to accommodate the needs of these male victims, hotline workers often infer that they must be the actual abusers and refer them to batterers' programs.[55]

In the judicial system, male victims of domestic violence are often treated unfairly solely because of their gender. Indeed, men who make claims of domestic violence face a deeply hostile system, which is far less sympathetic in its treatment of abused men. This is an area in which the "gender paradigm" has caused gross instances of injustice. In the United States, even with apparent corroborating evidence that their female partners were violent to them, male help-seekers often report that they lost child custody as a result of false accusations.[56] As noted by Professor Denise A. Hines (Psychology) and Dr Emily M. Douglas (Social Policy):

Male help-seekers have reported that their complaints concerning their female partners' violence have not always been taken seriously, yet their partner's false accusations have reportedly been given serious weight during the judicial process (Cook 1997). Other men have reported similar experiences in which their female partners misused the legal or social service systems to inappropriately block access between them and their children or to file false allegations with child welfare services (Hines et al 2007). According to some experts, the burden of proof for IPV [intimate partner violence] victimization is high for men because it falls outside of our common understanding of gender roles (Cook, 1997); this can make leaving a violent female partner that much more difficult. For example, many men who sustained IPV report that they stayed with their violent female partners in order to protect the children from their partner's violence. The men worried that if they left their violent wives, the legal system could still grant custody of the children to their wives and that perhaps even their custody rights would be blocked by their wives as a continuation of the controlling behaviours of their wives used during the marriage (McNeely et al, 2001)[57]

In the United States, an emergency clinic study in Ohio found that burns obtained in domestic relations were as frequent for male victims as for female victims, and that 72 per cent of men admitted with injuries from spousal violence had been stabbed.[58] Likewise, at an emergency clinic in Philadelphia male patients reported being kicked, bitten, punched or choked by female intimate partners in 47 per cent of cases. Unfortunately, such emergency clinics tend to ask only women, but never men, about potential domestic violence origins for injuries.[59]

This may be a natural consequence of the cornerstone of mainstream feminist theory that domestic violence is primarily motivated by "patriarchal control". According to Adam Blanch, a clinical psychologist and family counsellor working in Melbourne, "only a very small percentage of domestic violence is found to be motivated by control".[60] As he points out, "control" is a motive for both men and women in equal proportions. "An extraordinarily large body of evidence consistently shows that most domestic violence is committed by both women and men and is motivated by feelings of revenge, frustration and anger," he says.[61] His conclusion is that women are no less violent than men, although female violence against male partners is under-reported.

As Hines and Douglas comment in their seminal study on women's use of domestic violence against men, "the conceptualisation of domestic violence from a strict feminist viewpoint has hampered the ability of women who abuse their male partners to seek and get help from social service and criminal justice systems".[62] Women who resort to such violence face considerable barriers when seeking help within the current social service system. The following quote exemplifies the experience of one of these abusive women:

He tries to understand my side of the argument. He talks to me rather than hits me. I still hit him, however. I would like to enrol in a class in anger management, but the shelter for battered women does not help women with this problem[63]

Male victims struggle to locate anti-domestic violence services to assist them, since help lines or shelters are generally targeted towards female victims. They often report that their complaints concerning their female partners' violence have not been taken seriously.[64] Instead, male victims who have reached out to domestic violence organisations in the past have found themselves further abused by feminist services that refuse to believe that any man can be a victim of domestic violence. Some have even been put at risk of further violence not only against themselves but also against their children by these services contacting the abusing spouse and letting her know the man has sought help. There is even the assumption that the victim himself could actually be the perpetrator.

A psychiatrist who lives in Melbourne and once rang the Victorian "Men's Referral Service", commented: "I rang them on two occasions in relation to male victims. Both times I was told that if I had dug deeper I would have discovered that the men were the perpetrators." This shows that a supposedly public service provider is pushing the anti-male agenda of radical feminists. With so many Australian men taking their own lives, our governments have the moral duty to provide these abused men the help they so desperately need, particularly when family violence is concerned.

However, the New South Wales government has just gone the opposite direction. It has appointed a feminist organisation to assist male victims of domestic violence. This organisation's website says: "The Men's Referral Service (MRS) provides free, anonymous, and confidential telephone counselling, information, and referrals to men to assist them to take action to stop using violent and controlling behaviour."[65] It is unacceptable that information given "for men" is entirely predicated on men being the sole perpetrators of violence. The MRS is on the public record as saying services "need to be cautious in automatically assuming that a man assessed by police or another referring agent as a victim of domestic violence truly is the victim".[66] According to Greg Andresen, a spokesman for "One in Three Campaign", which advocates for male family violence victims:

A male victim seeking support who reads on a website that he needs to take responsibility for his "violent and controlling behaviour" is probably not going to have a lot of confidence in ringing that service and asking for help. And if he does call and is assumed responsible for the violence, he may not reach out for help again.[67]

Female domestic violence against children

The distortion of the truth is found also in discussions about domestic violence against children. "A quarter of Australian children had witnessed violence against their mother," South Australia's Victims of Crime Commissioner Michael O'Connell stated in August 2010. This statistic comes from "Young People and Domestic Violence", a study that reveals almost an identical proportion of young people being aware of female violence against their fathers or stepfathers.[68] The study found that, although 23 per cent of young Australians were aware of violence against their mothers or stepmothers, 22 per cent witnessed the same sort of violence against their fathers or stepfathers.[69] According to Bettina Arndt:

Whenever statistics are mentioned publicly that reveal the true picture of women's participation in family violence, they are dismissed with the domestic violence lobby claiming they are based on flawed methodology or are taken out of context. However, [according to] the best available quantitative data—ABS surveys, AIC (Australian Institute of Criminology) and homicide statistics—police crime data show that a third of victims of violence are males. These data sources are cited by the main domestic violence organisations, [although] they deliberately minimise any data relating to male victims.[70]

Many young Australians grow up afraid of their mothers. Australian children in violent families are more likely to be killed by their mothers than by their fathers. Although men made up a quarter of the 1645 partner deaths between 1989 and 2012, women accounted for 52 per cent of all child homicides. [71] Women not only are more likely to kill their children, but also account for more than half of all the substantial maltreatment perpetrators. In May 2015, the Australian Institute of Criminology released a research paper which states: "Where females were involved in a homicide, they were more likely to be the offender in a domestic/family homicide."[72] Although the majority of victims of domestic homicides overall were female (60 per cent), women were the sole offenders in more than half of the filicides (52 per cent) and offenders in 23 per cent of intimate partner homicides.[73] Also, men were more likely than their female partners to become the victims of filicide (56 per cent), parricide (54 per cent), and homicides involving other domestic relationships (70 per cent).[74]

Final Comments

Domestic violence used by women against men is a phenomenon that has received little attention from the Australian media and government. From the nation's media reports, public inquiries and official campaigns, one would believe that men are the sole perpetrators of domestic violence—and that all men are equally likely to carry out such acts of violence. Yet for nearly four decades research has shown that men are frequently the targets of violence by their female partners. Those who deny this evidence may resort to scientifically unacceptable tactics. This includes "concealing these results, selective citation of research, stating conclusions that are the opposite of the data, and even intimidating researchers who have produced results showing gender symmetry".[75]

I have no intention of minimising the real problem of serious domestic violence against women. One must speak out loud and clear about violence against women. In fact, we must speak out loud and clear about violence against *anyone*. This is why recognising that men are also victims of domestic violence is so important. Enough of pretending domestic violence is simply about dangerous men terrorising their families. It is time to abandon this sexist and harmful paradigm, and correct all the injustices caused by the politicisation of such a tragic reality that affects countless adults and children, male and female alike.

Dr Augusto Zimmermann is Professor of Law at Sheridan College in Perth, and Professor of Law (Adjunct) at the University of Notre Dame Australia, Sydney campus. He is also President of the Western Australian Legal Theory Association, and a former Commissioner with the Law Reform Commission of Western Australia.

[1] John Flint, "WA counsellor says he was forced to resign for domestic violence view', PerthNow, May 21, 2018, at https://www.perthnow.com.au/news/perth/wa-counsellor-says-he-was-forced-to-resign-for-domestic-violence-view-ng-b88838505z

[2] Bettina Arndt, "Domestic Violence: Data Shows Women are Not the Only Victims', *The Weekend Australian*, August 20, 2016, at https://www.theaustralian.com.au/news/inquirer/domestic-violence-data-shows-women-are-not-the-only-victims/news-story/2749c4517a57c33aca8bc2da9a40e2f9

[3] Flint, above n.1

[4] "Rob Tiller is an experienced, well-respected counsellor who worked for this counselling organisation for the past eight years. He was much in demand as the only male counsellor working in Perth, running their workshops in addition to seeing his clients … Tiller has taken RAWA to the Fair Work Commission claiming unfair dismissal. The organisation is claiming that Tiller wasn't dismissed but rather that he resigned. Yet he was told by the HR manager that he had to "resign or be fired" and that being fired would mean a black mark on his record. He took a day to formally resign but, in the meantime, the organisation cancelled his clients and told them he had already resigned". – Bettina Arndt, "The grip of feminist ideology on our key institutions', *The Spectator Australia*, May 12, 2018, at

https://www.spectator.com.au/2018/05/the-grip-of-feminist-ideology-on-our-key-institutions

[5] "In Brief: Domestic Violence: Not Always One Sided', *Harvard Medical School*, September 2007, at https://www.health.harvard.edu/newsletter_article/In_Brief_Dome stic_violence_Not_always_one_sided

[6] Daniel J. Whitaker PhD, Tadesse Haileysus MS, Monica Swahn PhD, and Linda S. Saltzman PhD, "Differences in Frequency of Violence and Reported Injury between Relationships with Reciprocal and Nonreciprocal Intimate Partner Violence" (2007) 97 (5) *American Journal of Public Health*, pp. 941–47. At the time of this study, Dr Daniel J. Whitaker and Dr Linda S. Saltzman were with the Division of Violence Prevention., National Centre for Injury Prevention and Control, Centres for Disease Control and Prevention, Atlanta/GA. Tadesse Haileyesus was with the Office of Statistics and Programming, National Centre for Injury Prevention and Control. Manica Swahn was with the Office on Smoking and Health, Centre for Disease, Control and Prevention.

[7] Ibid., at 941. See also: S.M. Smith, D.B. Smith, C.E. Penn, D.B. Ward, D. Tritt, "Intimate Partner Physical Abuse Perpetration and Victimization Risk Factors: A Meta-Analytic Review" (2004) 10 *Aggress Violent Behaviour* 65-98.

[8] Whitaker et al, above n.6, at 943.

[9] Ibid., at 943-44.

[10] Ibid., at 944.

[11] Ibid.

[12] Ibid.

[13] Ibid., at 941.

[14] Murray A. Straus, "Thirty Years of Denying the Evidence on Gender Symmetry in Partner Violence: Implications for Prevention and Treatment" (2010) 1 *Partner Abuse* 332, at 333.

[15] "Perhaps the most frequent method of dealing with the unacceptable evidence that women assault partners at the same or higher rate as men is to conceal the evidence. The pattern was established early in research on PV by a survey conducted for the Kentucky Commission on Women (Schulman, 1979). This excellent survey found about equal rates of assault by men and women partners, but only assaults by men were presented in the commission report". – Straus, above n.14, at 339.

[16] Bettina Arndt, "Flirting with Confected Outrage Fails to Impress Women', *The Australian*, 7 January, 2016, at https://www.theaustralian.com.au/opinion/flirting-with-confected-outrage-fails-to-impress-women/news-story/13b5e0c486c037fce7f0a3fd625f801b

[17] Christian Porter, "Women's Safety Package Set to Stop the Violence', Media Release, 25 September 2015, at http://www.christianporter.com.au/womens-safety-package-set-to-stop-the-violence/

[18] Peter O'Brien, "Home Truths About Domestic Violence', *Quadrant Magazine*, n.4, 2016, at https://quadrant.org.au/181115/opinion/qed/2016/04/home-truths-domestic-violence/

[19] Angela Shanahan, "Domestic Violence Beat Up', *The Spectator Australia*, November 10, 2015

[20] Malcolm Turnbull, "Reducing Violence Against Women and their Children', Joint Press Conference, November 25, 2015, at http://www.malcolmturnbull.com.au/media/joint-press-conference-release-of-the-report-reducing-violence-against-wome

[21] Chip Le Grand, "Resident Evil: Women Rare Victims on Streets', *The Weekend Australian*, June 23, 2018, p 10.

[22] Ibid.

[23] Claire Lehmann, "One Man Killed Eurydice But All Are Held To Account', *The Weekend Australian*, June 23, 2018, p 21.

[24] Ibid.

[25] Arndt, above n.16.

[26] Linda Mills, *Insult to Injury: Rethinking our Responses to Intimate Abuse* (Princeton University Press, 2003), at 8.

[27] Erin Pizzey, "Why I loathe feminism... and believe it will ultimately destroy the family', *Daily Mail*, 24 September 2009, at http://www.dailymail.co.uk/femail/article-1215464/Why-I-loathe-feminism—believe-

[28] Ibid.

[29] Ibid.

[30] See: Alicia Spidel, Caroline Greaves, Tonia L. Nicholls, Julie Goldenson, Donald G Dutton, "Personality Disorders, Types of Violence, and Stress Responses in Female Who Perpetrate Intimate Partner Violence" (2013) 4 *Psychology* 5-11; See also: Donald G Dutton and Katherine White, "Male Victims of Domestic Violence" (2013) 2 (1) *New Male Studies* 5-17; See also: Denise A. Hines and Emily M. Douglas, "Women's Use of Intimate Partner Violence against Men: Prevalence, Implications and Consequences (2009) 18 *Journal of Aggression, Maltreatment & Trauma* 572-586. See also: Denise A. Hines and Kathleen Malley-Morrison, "Psychological Effects of Partner Abuse Against

Men: A Neglected Research Area" (2001) 2 (2) *Psychology of Men & Masculinity* 75-85.

[31] Murray A. Straus, "Thirty Years of Denying the Evidence on Gender Symmetry in Partner Violence: Implications for Prevention and Treatment" (2010) 1 *Partner Abuse* 332

[32] Straus, above n.14.

[33] Ibid., at 337.

[34] Ibid, at 338.

[35] Denise A. Hines and Emily M. Douglas, "Women's Use of Intimate Partner Violence Against Men: Prevalence, Implications and Consequences" 18 (2009) *Journal of Aggression, Maltreatment & Trauma* 572, at 572.

[36] R .J. Gelles, *The Violent Home: A Study of Physical Aggression Between Husbands and Wives* (Beverly Hills/CA: Sage, 1974), at 77.

[37] Ibid, at 151.

[38] Denis Campbell, "More Than 40% of Domestic Violence Victims Are Male, Report Reveals". *The Guardian*, September 5th, 2010, at https://www.theguardian.com/society/2010/sep/05/men-victims-domestic-violence

[39] Antonia Hoyle, "Why are so many men become victims of Domestic Violence? It's one of Britain's Last Remaining Taboos, but Abuse Against Men in the Home is on the Rise', Daily Mail, 5 December 2013

[40] Ibid.

[41] Ibid.

[42] Denis Campbell, "More Than 40% of Domestic Violence Victims Are Male, Report Reveals". The Guardian, September 5th, 2010, at https://www.theguardian.com/society/2010/sep/05/men-victims-domestic-violence

[43] Denis Campbell, "More Than 40% of Domestic Violence Victims Are Male, Report Reveals". The Guardian, September 5th, 2010, at https://www.theguardian.com/society/2010/sep/05/men-victims-domestic-violence Even so, in Britain alone, the number of women prosecuted for domestic violence rose from 1,575 in 2004-05 to 4,266 in 2008-09

[44] Arndt, above n.16.

[45] Hines & Douglas, above n.36, at 574. See also: M. Henman, "Domestic Violence: Do Men Under Report? (1998) 47 *Forensic Update* 3-8.

[46] Ibid., at 574. See also: S. K. Steinmetz, "Wifebeating, Husbandbeating: A Comparison of the Use of Physical Violence Between Spouses to Resolve Marital Fights', in M. Roy (ed.), *Battered Women: Psychosociological Study of Domestic Violence* (New York/NY: Van Nostrand Reinhold Co, 1977), at 63-72.

[47] S.W. Mihalic & D. Elliott, "If Violence is Domestic, Does it Really Count" (1997) 12 *Journal of Family Violence* 293-311.

[48] Donald G. Dutton and Katherine R. White, "Male Victims of Domestic Violence', (2013) 2 (1) *New Male Studies* 5, at 8.

[49] Hines & Douglas, above n.36, at 573.; See also: R.L. McNeely, P.W. Cook & J.B. Torres, "Is Domestic Violence a Gender Issue, or a Human Issue?'(2001) 4 *Journal of Human Behaviour in the Social Environment* 227-251.

[50] Hines & Douglas, above n.36, at 578.

[51] Sotirios Sarantakos, "Deconstructing Self-Defense in Wife-to-Husband Violence', (2004) 12 (3) *The Journal of Men's Studies* 277, 287

[52] K Henning and B Renauer, "Prosecution of Women Arrested for Intimate Partner Abuse', (2005) 20 (3) *Violence and Victims* 361-373.

[53] Hines & Douglas, above n.36, at 578.

[54] "Fighting False Allegations of Domestic Violence', HG.org, at http://hg.org/article.asp?id=6008

[55] Ibid.

[56] Hines & Douglas, above n.36, at 579.

[57] Ibid.

[58] Ibid., at 572.

[59] Ibid, at 10.

[60] Adam Blanch, "The Fallacious Stereotype of "Male Violence', and Why It's Being Sold to You', *On Line Opinion – Australia's E-Journal of Social and Political Debate*, at www.onlineopinion.com.au/print.asp?article=16394

[61] Ibid.

[62] Hines & Douglas, above n.36, at 573.

[63] W.A. Stacey, L.R. Hazlewood & A. Shupe, *The Violence Couple* (Westport/CT: Praeger, 1994), p 63.

[64] Denise A. Hines & Emily M. Douglas, "A Closer Look at Men who Sustain Intimate Terrorism by Women', (2010) 1 (3) *Partner Abuse* 286-313

[65] "About the Men's Referral Service', *Men's Referral Service*, at http://mrs.org.au/about/

[66] "No To Violence Response to the One in Three Organisation's Comments about Male Victims', *No To Violence & Men's Referral Service*, at http://ntv.org.au/wp-content/uploads/141125-senate-dv-inquiry-NTV-1in3campaign-response.pdf

[67] "Appointment of feminist group to aid male family violence victims "a curious choice"', *One in Three*, November 8th 2016, at

http://www.oneinthree.com.au/news/2016/11/8/appointment-of-feminist-group-to-aid-male-family-violence-vi.html

[68] Arndt, above n.16.

[69] "Young People and Domestic Violence: National Research of Young People's Attitudes to and Experiences of Domestic Violence', *Commonwealth of Australia – Attorney-General's Department*, Canberra/ACT, September 2001.

[70] Ibid.

[71] Tracy Cussen and Willow Bryant, "Domestic/Family Homicide in Australia', Australian Institute of Criminology, No.38, May 2015, at 2.

[72] Ibid., at 3.

[73] Ibid.

[74] Ibid.,

[75] "Perhaps the most frequent method of dealing with the unacceptable evidence that women assault partners at the same or higher rate as men is to conceal the evidence. The pattern was established early in research on PV by a survey conducted for the Kentucky Commission on Women (Schulman, 1979). This excellent survey found about equal rates of assault by men and women partners, but only assaults by men were presented in the commission report". – Straus, above n.14, at 339.

Even the briefest of perusals of the above paper should give the reader more of an insight into the problem faced by men who are victims of domestic violence. It struck a chord in me, as I could see in the writing all of the problems I had experienced in my own marriage.

In my search for the truth, I have come upon a number of research papers and articles on the subject of women perpetrating domestic violence on men. I found the most comprehensive was a reference paper:

'Reference Examining Assaults by Women on their Spouses or Male Partners,' by Martin Fiebert, Department of Psychology, University of California. (2)

This article examines 343 scholarly investigations; 270 empirical studies and 73 reviews and/or analyses, which demonstrate women are as physically aggressive, or more aggressive, than men in their relationships with their spouses or male partners. The aggregate sample size in the reviewed studies exceeds 440,850 people. The papers are from the USA and around the world, including some from England, South Africa, Australia and New Zealand. Most of the references in the paper date from the 1980's through to 2013. Most are relatively recent.

It is an eye opening experience to read through the findings of these studies and reviews and see the results of so many in-depth investigations into relationships and attitudes. Some facts are gleaned from FBI murder investigations of domestic violence deaths while other results come from information obtained through hospitals. At times the figures make grim reading. Throughout all of the papers, the take home message is that women are responsible for initiating violence in nearly fifty percent of cases. There are varying degrees of violence recorded, from a light slap right through to murder. From the research, which is not biased and is also peer reviewed, it appears that this violence is not just in self defence as is often claimed but that it is also initiated by women.

The other fact that seems to run throughout the writing is that women suffer serious injury more often than men. In my opinion I believe that to be a result of a number of factors, foremost among them retaliation by men who have initially been assaulted by the woman in the relationship. It can be an immediate retaliation to a violent act or something which builds up over many years of being physically abused to be released in one explosive outburst. Whatever it is, the results are similar. Men tend to be larger and more physically powerful than women and are generally able to inflict more physical damage. A lot of numbers for the statistics in various research papers and reports are gleaned from medical records. Another possible reason for the greater number of women appearing in the statistics, one often overlooked, is that men are reluctant to seek medical attention after domestic wounding and also tend to lie about the cause of it due to the embarrassment and possible repercussions. A further reason for more women presenting for treatment in the first place could be the need for clinical records to provide evidence for obtaining a DVO.

I am not trying to lessen the seriousness of the situation regarding injury to female victims of domestic violence but rather to point out that there is a possibility of error. It is an area that needs to be addressed to find the truth of the matter. As an example I will quote a recent newspaper article. "Women being treated in emergency departments will be asked question's about their partner's behaviour, in an Australian-first trial to tackle domestic violence. Up to 75,000 women aged between 16 and 65, will be screened in the government program to be piloted in six NSW hospitals". There is no mention of male victims or of males being asked the same question, although we know at least 25% of the victims of domestic violence are male. These men are totally ignored in nearly every official action taken to combat 'the scourge of domestic violence'. The article goes on to say, "The NSW Minister for the Prevention of Domestic Violence, Pru Goward, said the project was designed to reach more women needing help". What about the men who need help?

The ratio of deaths at the hands of a partner from domestic violence is variably quoted depending on the source of information but generally, more women die at the hands of their male partner than the reverse. What is surprising is the number of men who are killed by their female partners, around 20% or one fifth of total domestic violence deaths in Australia. Far more than we are led to believe.

However, as previously discussed, most of the people who need to read this extensive list of references and digest the facts as well as help disseminate them, have no interest in doing so. The actual facts fly in the face of the currently held feminist, moralistic and somewhat Marxist viewpoint and as such will be ignored by those very people whose duty it is to report 'news'. It seems, like their counterparts in an abusive relationship, many men in the industry are running scared of their female opposite numbers and the possible negative fallout from their female audiences if they expressed views counter to the current popularly held ones regarding domestic violence.

The Australian Government's, Australian Institute of Health and Welfare Report on Family, domestic and sexual violence in Australia 2018, sets out to report on all these figures and is probably quoted quite often as a Government benchmark for domestic violence in Australia.

It states,

"The Australian Institute of Health and Welfare is a major national agency whose purpose is to create authoritative and accessible information and statistics that inform decisions and improve the health and welfare of *all* Australians (italics mine).

Unfortunately, in my opinion, this report is biased toward female victims of domestic violence which is unfortunate, as the report could have been a fair and reliable guide to what is actually occurring in Australia. Its bias also makes the plight of male victims all the more insidious as an actual Government publication, purporting to report facts, is weakening the case for fairer outcomes for the many men who are victims of domestic violence.

The Acknowledgement section of the document lists the authors of the report, its funding and expert advice. I have reproduced it in full below.

Acknowledgments

This report was written by Ms Ann Hunt, Ms Karen Webber, Ms Jennaya Montgomery and Ms Amy Duong from the Australian Institute of Health and Welfare (AIHW),

with assistance from Ms Karen Hobson, Ms Kate Riley Sandler, Mr Mark Cooper-Stanbury, Ms Jenni Joenpera, Mr Andrew Ticehurst and Ms Miriam Lum On.

The contributions of reviewers from the AIHW, including Ms Louise York, Dr Lynelle Moon, Mr Matthew James, Dr Fadwa Al-Yaman, Mr Geoff Neideck and Mr Barry Sandison, are also acknowledged.

The contributions of funders, including the Department of Social Services, the Victorian Department of Premier and Cabinet, the New South Wales Department of Premier and Cabinet, the Department of the Prime Minister and Cabinet, and the Australian Capital Territory Justice and Community Safety Directorate are gratefully acknowledged, as is the expert advice provided by the advisory group established for the report, whose members are:

Dr Peta Cox Australia's National Research Organisation for Women's Safety

Mr Stephen Collett Australian Bureau of Statistics

Mr Will Milne Australian Bureau of Statistics

Ms Anthea Saflekos Australian Bureau of Statistics

Ms Jo Wood Australian Capital Territory Justice and Community Safety Directorate

Dr Samantha Bricknell Australian Institute of Criminology

Mr Anthony Morgan Australian Institute of Criminology

Ms Kelly Hand Australian Institute of Family Studies

Ms Lixia Qu Australian Institute of Family Studies

Ms Rose Beynon Department of Social Services

Dr Marian Esler Department of Social Services

Ms Rachel Livingston Department of the Prime Minister and Cabinet

Ms Tarja Saastamoinen Department of the Prime Minister and Cabinet

Ms Kirsti Van Der Steen Department of the Prime Minister and Cabinet

Ms Jenna Palumbo New South Wales Department of Premier and Cabinet

Ms Bethany Fenech Victorian Department of Premier and Cabinet

The authors would also like to thank the following people for their valuable input:

Ms Marilyn Chilvers New South Wales Department of Family and Community Services

Prof Deb Loxton The University of Newcastle

Ms Debra Reid The University of Sydney

Dr Michael Salter Western Sydney University

It can be seen that most of the authors and people involved with the preparation of this report are women. I have, in the past, read a lot of material authored by women, both scientific and non scientific and I am well aware that women can and do, write excellent, unbiased and informative scientific reports and articles. However, scrutiny of this particular document reveals the use of emotive language and emotive descriptions in a number of places throughout. Emotive language has no place in a supposedly unbiased report. The first paragraph of the introduction states, 'Although men are victims of domestic violence and sexual assault, most victims are women." This statement combines two different data sets, one regarding domestic violence, which is defined here as occurring between intimate or once intimate partners and sexual assault, which may often and does occur between people who don't know each other and far more often to women than men. Combining these two separate pieces of data into a single conclusion effectively manipulates known facts and obfuscates the evidence regarding men on the receiving end of domestic violence. Further on, beneath a graphic showing that ninety nine women and twenty seven men were killed by a current or previous partner between 2012 and 2014 there is the statement, "Most family, domestic and sexual violence is against women, by men." Once again, family and sexual violence, not necessarily a part of domestic violence is used to cloud the issue here, as a lot of sexual violence occurs outside of relationships. It is an inflammatory statement considering the graphic above it illustrates just over 22% or one fifth of *total* partner deaths were perpetrated by women on their current or previous male partner. This should not be a minor detail to be overlooked and buried in emotive statements and would not be, in a fair and equitable report.

On page seven the report states, "As many data collections focus on violence perpetrated by an intimate partner, particularly male violence against women, much of this report focuses on domestic violence." Note the 'particularly male violence against women' inserted into the statement.

On page twelve we have the results of the NCAS - National Community Attitudes towards Violence Against Women Survey, held three times over the years by the Victorian Government. No mention of a 'Violence against Men Survey', that subject is behind the dark curtain. However, the ABS Personal Safety Survey of 2016 does report that nationally 4.8% of women and 4.2% of men experienced emotional abuse by their partners in the preceding twelve months. As emotional abuse is universally recognised as domestic violence, this fact should be included in any survey. These figures show 47% of this form of domestic violence is perpetrated by women on men but we don't hear a word about it in the news or publications, the information is left out so as to make a case for women only.

Yet again, on page thirty two is the sub heading, "Domestic violence is *predominantly* perpetrated by males." Yet above it, on page thirty one the info graphic shows 25%

or one quarter of the victims of domestic violence reported the perpetrator as female.

Another anomaly is the term 'family violence' which has little to do with 'domestic violence' being used in some of the overall figures. There is an assumption made here that family violence is also perpetrated mostly by males but this is not necessarily the case, although that point is not made. Women abusing children, old people being abused and other forms of abuse are all included in family violence figures. In the NSW Police Force document, 'Domestic and Family Violence Policy' from 2017, a figure of 37% is given for family violence not pertaining to couples in a relationship.

Rather than continuing to point out emotive references in this document, I will concentrate on another source of statistical inaccuracy. This survey used data from recorded crime offenders and victims, plus data from the criminal courts. As we shall see shortly, men under-report domestic violence to authorities and women are dealt with far more leniently by the courts, often having no conviction recorded. This influences the data. There also appears to be plenty of data available for women's partners being charged but the authors of the above report could find *no* corresponding data for men's female partners being charged. Why I wonder? It should be readily available, the same as the data for men is. Moreover, specialist homelessness services seem unable to separate data on the number of men versus the number of women being assisted after a domestic violence incident; possibly because men don't often 'qualify' for assistance after a domestic violence incident.

Statistics are funny things and a lot of misinformation can be presented by the inaccurate use of figures. Results often depend on how groupings and exclusions are handled in the analysis. Mark Twain, a well known American author, is often quoted as saying, "There are lies, damn lies and statistics."

Besides continually mentioning violence against women and the fact men are responsible for it, *The Australian Government's, Australian Institute of Health and Welfare Report on Family, domestic and sexual violence in Australia 2018* also uses population data sets which possibly include figures from Indigenous Australians who suffer from a significantly greater proportion of domestic and family violence. If this information *is* included it would tend to skew results, misrepresenting figures for the rest of the population. However, separate specific figures are given for Indigenous Australians in the last quarter of the report. The report also lumps sexual violence in with domestic violence giving the impression that this sexual violence is taking place in a domestic situation when in fact the data relates to sexual violence in general which is also perpetrated throughout the community at large.

Remember, we are talking about *The Australian Government's, Australian Institute of Health and Welfare Report on Family, domestic and sexual violence in Australia 2018*, a document no doubt used in making major policy decisions, possibly having a negative affect on the outcomes for male victims of domestic violence.

Another interesting observation in this report, which is not reflected in research from around the world, is that women's violence in relationships is not increasing in Australia. This runs counter to the findings in a paper, *Relationship Aggression, Violence & Self Regulation in Australian Newlyweds, by Halford W.K. et al 2010.* One of its conclusions is that women's violence is increasing.

It is my opinion that *The Australian Government's,*

Australian Institute of Health and Welfare Report on Family, domestic and sexual violence in Australia 2018 suffers from the widely held Government viewpoint that men are solely responsible for domestic violence because it is a *gendered crime*. This is definitely a case of misandry but I hear no outcries and the Government is protected from its own anti discrimination laws (see later) when these claims are made. This viewpoint is very pervasive throughout society, using the outdated, historical Patriarchal Dominance model and can result in 'no platforming' for any articles on female domestic violence against males in any Government material printed on the subject of domestic violence. This is partially a result of the *'National Plan to Reduce Violence against Women and their Children 2010-2022'*. While I applaud the Government implementing such a plan, I find it very strange that men, in the face of so much evidence to the contrary, have been completely excluded from a National Plan purported to address domestic violence. The way the, *'National Plan to Reduce Violence against Women and their Children 2010-2022'* operates results in a distinct lack of funding for researchers who may want to explore a broader viewpoint of domestic violence and get to the truth of the matter. Likewise, all the Government advertising models blame only men for domestic violence and the Government's own report from the Australian Institute of Health and Welfare unfortunately goes a long way towards echoing those views.

A couple of years ago I worked at a radio station for a few days a week and happened to answer the phone one day after everyone had gone home. Someone on the other end had received a grant from the Government to publicise Domestic Violence and wanted to buy advertising airspace. I asked him, 'off the record' if that advertising would also mention domestic violence perpetrated by women against men. His answer - "No, the Government would only give out a grant to publicise domestic violence against women perpetrated by men."

The Victorian State Government supported, 'The Lookout – Fact sheet 7 – Family violence statistics', is yet another example of bias. It talks almost exclusively about women and violence against them, quoting only scientific articles which are studies of violence against women. Under the heading, Prevalence, it states. "There are high rates of family violence in Australia. Most cases involve men abusing their female partners." How can they honestly make this statement in light of all the research data presently available, which paints an entirely different picture to that which they are portraying? This is supposed to be a 'fact' sheet. Victoria is also responsible for a telephone referral service solely for males who are thinking of, or have committed acts of domestic violence. Male *victims* of domestic violence have, on numerous occasions, also been referred to this site for counselling because it seems to be common knowledge in Victoria that domestic violence is a gendered crime and only men commit domestic violence. There is no such site for female domestic violence perpetrators. Officially, there doesn't seem to be any female perpetrators of domestic violence in Victoria.

The NSW Police, Domestic and Family Violence Policy 2018, is written in a non emotive manner. It is factual in its discussion and aims to provide information on the policing of domestic and family violence. In that document there is mention of support given to victims of domestic violence under the 'Safer Pathways' program.

"Under Safer Pathway once a police officer completes the DVSAT it is automatically, electronically referred to the Central Referral Point (CRP), an electronic platform operated by Victims Services. Based on the gender and location of the victim, the CRP then on-refers the victim to receive local specialist support services. Female victims are referred to a Women's Domestic Violence Court Advocacy Service (WDVCAS) and in sites where Safer Pathway has been rolled out, to a Local Coordination Point (LCP) for follow up and support. *Male victims are referred to a local specialist service providing telephone advice, counselling, support and referral for male victims.*" (Italics by author.) This is, once again, official discrimination against male victims of domestic violence, something which will be covered later.

Although approximately 20% (according to some official figures – the actual incidence is more likely to be at least 25%) of domestic violence is directed toward men by women, support for these male victims is a telephone call only? Is it any wonder the suicide rate of male victims of domestic violence is so high? Appendix 2 of the same policy report states:

"We acknowledge firstly that most men are not violent, abusive or controlling; and secondly that men can also be victims of family violence."

In my research I came across an excellent Australian Government publication, *'Australian Institute of Criminology, Research Report 13, Policing domestic violence: A review of the evidence 2018'.* The report is up to date and exceedingly well authored. It reviews a vast swathe of literature and is non discriminatory in its approach. There are a number of points this report makes which are germane to this discussion and quoted here.

Page IX 'Victims are less likely to report when they are male, white, young, living with the perpetrator, and from a higher socio-economic background'.

'Similarly, (in reference to arrests) victim and perpetrator gender, ethnicity, relationship type and age also show mixed results'.

Page XII 'Police are under increasing pressure to lay

evidence-driven as opposed to victim-driven charges, meaning that factors beyond the desires of the victim are prioritised in the decision to charge (or not). However, the heavy reliance on victim statements as evidence, and the difficulty of obtaining these where victims do not support prosecution, can hamper evidence-driven charging'.

Page 21 'Domestic violence involving *female victims* is more likely to be reported to police both by the victims themselves (Dugan 2003; Felson et al. 2002; Kang & Lynch 2010; Kingsnorth & MacIntosh 2004; MacQueen & Norris 2016; Mirrlees-Black 1999) and by third-parties (Felson & Paré 2005) *than domestic violence involving male victims* (italics mine). Male victims may feel embarrassment or discomfort discussing abuse by a female partner, believe that they should be able to manage the situation without police intervention, or simply not recognise that they are victims of abuse. Felson et al. (2002) also found that male victims of female perpetrators frequently consider their abuse to be trivial'.

Page 47 'There is also limited evidence to suggest that male perpetrators are more likely to be arrested, while no conclusive results have emerged regarding officer characteristics or victim and perpetrator gender, ethnicity, relationship type or age.'

This is a Government document which refreshingly deals with the facts without an agenda. No Patriarchal Dominance theory applied here and no socialist or feminist overtones, merely facts. Facts are important and are unfortunately overlooked or painted over when being morally right is more important than being factually correct.

All is not lost in this search for the truth in the Antipodes. Below are reproduced five research papers with an Australian authorship. When data is dissected without a bias to either gender, it can be demonstrated that the problem is not as simple as 'men are responsible for domestic violence'. Also, the simplification that women commit domestic violence only in self defence is also a myth, one perpetrated by women themselves in an effort to control outcomes.

Halford, W. K., Farrugia, C., Lizzio, A., & Wilson, K. (2010). Relationship aggression, violence and self-regulation in Australian newlywed couples. *Australian Journal of Psychology, 62*(2), 82-92. (A sample of 379 newlywed couples in Australia responded to a short version of the CTS. Results reveal that 22% of couples experienced a least one act of physical violence in the past year. Female perpetration of violence was more common that male perpetration. Authors report that in violence couples the more common pattern was for women to be violent <59%> followed by violence by both partners <34%> and least common was violence by men only <7%>).

Headey, B., Scott, D., & de Vaus, D. (1999). Domestic violence in Australia: Are women and men equally violent? Data from the International Social Science Survey/ Australia 1996/97 was examined. A sample of 1643 subjects (804 men, 839 women) responded to questions about their experience with domestic violence in the past 12 months. Results reveal that 5.7% of men and 3.7% of women reported being victims of domestic assaults. With regard to injuries results reveal that women inflict serious injuries at least as frequently as men. For example 1.8% of men and 1.2% of women reported that their injuries required first aid, while 1.5% of men and 1.1% of women reported that their injuries needed treatment by a doctor or nurse.

Lewis, A. & Sarantakos, S. (2001). Domestic Violence and the male victim. *Nuance, #3.* (Based on interviews with 48 men in Australia and New Zealand, authors present findings that domestic violence by women toward men exists, that the refusal to examine the prevalence of this abuse is a "disempowerment" of men and that official policy should be changed to provide help for abused men.)

Sarantakos, S. (2004). Deconstructing self-defense in wife-to-husband violence. *Journal of Men's Studies, 12* (3) 277-296. (Members of 68 families with violent wives in Australia were studied. In 78% of cases wives' violence was reported to be moderate to severe and in 38% of cases husbands needed medical attention. Using information from husbands, wives, children and wives' mothers study provides compelling data challenging self-defense as a motive for female-to-male violence.)

Stockdale, G. L. (1998). *Men's Accounts of Domestic Violence.* Unpublished master's thesis. Deakin University, Australia. (Twenty male victims of domestic violence were interviewed using a semi-structured protocol. Many subjects incurred severe physical violence and were "mostly disturbed by false accusations of violence on their part, and their partner's use of their children against them, which they felt were supported by the legal system and the community.")

Look at the dates of these articles. Some have been around for twenty years and no one seems to have bothered to incorporate these results in any modern program to assist male victims of domestic violence.

In a newspaper article in a National newspaper, Glen Poole, the CEO of the Australian Men's Health Forum says, "Research by the Australian Men's Health Forum has found men die six years younger then women; three in four suicides are men; boys are 60% more likely to drop out of school by Year 12; men account for 92% of workplace deaths and 72% of work–related disease; only five percent of primary parental leave is taken by dads; about 2 million men experience economic insecurity; one in four men are socially isolated; and most government initiatives to tackle gender issues focus on women and children". He goes on to say. "According to researchers at the University of Canberra, the majority of Australians support equality between men and women, but are concerned that men and boys are increasingly excluded from measures to improve gender equality."

We all hear about the women's movement wanting gender equality but they don't seem to hand it out. We all hear about fairness but the media promotes a socialistic, moralistic and very biased viewpoint in favour of women. Men in the media have to get on board with that same message or they are labelled 'sexist' or 'misogynistic' as are politicians who don't toe the line. Many politicians worry about their popularity and don't want to risk any negative publicity, so knowingly perpetrate the myth of 'only men are abusers'. Recently Pauline Hanson, a One Nation Senator raised the point of men being unfairly dealt with in domestic violence outcomes and was the recipient of abuse from the public and negative publicity by the media. The worst thing of all is how the Law, which used to require proof of wrongdoing before convictions, is now accepting a woman's account of violence and/or sexual misconduct (victim statement) and finding men guilty solely on their wife or partner's or even a stranger's say so. What happened to evidence based decision making and innocent until proven guilty?

THE PRINCIPLES

Some of the following will be generalisations, as I'm not an anthropologist or psychologist or any other 'ogist'. This chapter is drawn from my own observations and extensive general reading over a period of many years.

The main driver for domestic violence seems to be an attempt to manipulate the other person in the relationship. Control means that one partner can dictate events, spending, distribution of assets, sex, friends or any one of a number of other items. The little women can be kept at home waiting or the husband can be stripped of his wage as he walks through the door. Often it's more subtle than that. Who has the credit cards, where we go when we go out, who has use of the car or whether we visit friends alone or always together. The battlefield is constantly changing but the underlying precepts remain the same.

In the initial phases of a relationship, and here I'll concentrate on women, there is an intuitive stage which women excel at. It has been shown that even by smell alone, women unconsciously tend to generally choose the provider type of male for partners, saving the testosterone hunks for when they are ovulating. What that means is that a woman who wants to take the *lead* role (not necessarily from the front) in a relationship will generally look for a 'nice' man. He is usually polite, deferential, often kind and likes animals, although that's not a necessary prerequisite. This is a man who can be manipulated and the woman who is juggling to be top dog in a relationship requires that. There seems to be an ability in some women to find males who can be coerced into doing whatever they want, and if not actually coerced then subtly manipulated. Even the testosterone types can fall into this category.

Domestic violence is not only physical though. Verbal abuse is also a form of violence.

Over the years I have had a small number of relationships and eventually abandoned each one when some of these signs of coercion or manipulation surfaced, especially when accompanied by 'firm' speech. I've been at the coal face once and have no desire to return there. In each case I've given ground for the sake of domestic harmony until I recognised the signs that I've been subtly and sometimes less than subtly, coerced into again doing what the other person wants without any discussion aimed at reaching a mutual understanding. Then I leave rather than enter into a domestic struggle. In most cases there seems to be a lack of respect. That's the magic word in all of these situations. Respect.

If you respect someone as a person, the idea of controlling them is quite alien. I often feel sorry for Bonsai trees as they are pruned and contorted into shape. They make me think of domestic violence and manipulation. Snip a bit here, cut a bit there then wrap with wire and bend into shape. Yes, the little trees do look amazing but that should never happen to a human being.

Once a relationship has begun and time, effort and energy has been invested in it, the idea of then splitting up is a difficult one, emotionally as well as financially. The perpetrators of domestic violence seem to know when the relationship has arrived at the stage where coercion can be applied. At first the coercion is subtle but then becomes less so as time wears on. The question is often asked of victims.

"Why did you stay?"

The answer is a very complex one depending on the circumstances but to the victim it is always a rational one.

"It only happens sometimes."

"I love my kids and don't want to leave them."

"If I do what she/he wants it will be alright."

"It's my fault for annoying/upsetting her/him."

"I should have remembered (the event, shopping, gift etc)."

"He/she only does it when he/she drinks."

"It's that time of the month."

"I should have come home earlier."

"She's a good mother to the kids."

The list is endless but they are all justifications for unnecessary violence. Similarly, the lists of the perpetrators is just as long. At times I wonder about the Stockholm Syndrome, a well known condition where an imprisoned kidnap victim falls in love with their captor.

Once children, a mortgage or joint finances enter the equation it becomes far more difficult for a man to leave a situation where he is being abused. The system is set up for women in spite of some of the alarming figures showing men are the victims of domestic violence in well over 25% of cases although interestingly, official figures gleaned from courts and arrest figures manage to show far less.

No safe houses for men.

Nowhere to escape the little women with your children.

What! A restraining order but you're a man, why would you need it?

Call the police? If necessary, but your spouse could point the finger while crying copious tears and you'd possibly be locked up. The problem is that many police act on what the woman tells them. Not the man. (Remember victim statements?) I've been in a similar position and that was thirty five years ago. Not that much has changed, although there are signs evidence based policing and arrests are becoming more common.

So you manage to get away from her. Eventually you will find that you have to pay child support even though you were driven out of your own house. And also have to pay toward the mortgage. If you are lucky you might get to see your children, that is of course unless your ex wife charges you with being a child molester/wife beater. In which case forget it.

There is also the matter of the AVO (DVO) which stops you going within half a kilometre of your family, taken out on your ex wife's word alone. (Victim statements again)

The above may be worst case scenarios, or not. It's a bit like a game of Russian Roulette, you just don't know what the outcome will be once you need to rely on the system for help. Whatever the outcome, it's really out of your hands and all you can do is repeat your story. However, for a male victim of domestic violence the punishment just keeps getting heaped on them, even after they are forced out of their home. I'm not making this up. The Tillbrook report from 2010 interviewed male victims of domestic abuse and looked into all the areas mentioned above. I have reproduced some of the conclusions below.

This huge disparity in outcomes is one of the drivers of male suicides. Nowhere to turn, no one to help and definitely no light at the end of the tunnel. I speak from experience, I've looked down that tunnel on many occasions, often through the distortion of the bottom of a bottle and it's not a pleasant view. Personally, I was strong enough and determined enough to survive, although the alcohol took its toll until I quit it. A lot of men aren't strong enough and in their despair choose to end their own life. This is a good outcome for the partner who was dishing out the violence. They milk the occasion for sympathy and are seen as the poor victim of an aggressive relationship with an essentially weak, mentally ill partner.

Another thing I've observed and talked to other abused men about is the fact that the female perpetrator of domestic violence nearly always assumes the role of the victim. This seems to garner sympathy from other women who also start treating the actual male victim with other than respect. As a man, trying to discuss domestic violence with anyone in your circle of male acquaintances is a difficult proposition. There is often disbelief, amusement, ridicule, the chance of being told to grow a pair, advice on fighting back and straight out derision. Double jeopardy. You not only get the violence from your partner but no help either. You're on your own Mate! It's far better to ring a Helpline and at least talk to someone before you reach that position.

However, no matter how horrible the woman is and how much evil she has levelled at the man, there is always someone to help the poor woman (victim) out. Government Departments and organisations fall over themselves to offer the victim help. I'm not saying this shouldn't be so but scattered among the genuine victims of domestic violence are the she wolves who take as much as they can get, as their right, with no conscience at all.

As far back as 2010, a research project commissioned by the Men's Advisory Network (MAN) and conducted by researchers of Edith Cowan University in Western Australia, who interviewed both male victims of domestic violence and social workers and organisations tasked with helping victims of domestic violence recognised the difficulties facing men in this situation. I have reproduced below both 'Some Final Issues' and 'Recommendations' from the original. The IPA referred to in the article stands for Intimate Partner Abuse

From: **'Intimate Partner Abuse of Men'**

by Emily Tillbrook et al. 2010

Edith Cowan University

6.2 Some Final Issues

As with other forms of family violence, gender is an important issue in men's victimisation. Regardless of what research eventually determines to be the similarities and the differences between men's and women's experiences as victims of IPA (not only in terms of prevalence and severity, but also support services and other responses to the violence and effective prevention of IPA), it is clear that gender issues need to be comprehensively examined. Since issues of power and control in relationships and gendered identity are relevant to male victims' experiences, feminist analyses of violence might be just as important in understanding men's experiences of IPA as they have proved to be in understanding women's experiences.

However, issues of masculinity and men's place in society must be examined broadly within a range of both psychological and sociological theories. Our data suggest that some of the perceived gender-biases that prevent men from disclosing their abuse (e.g., that he will be seen to have failed as a man if not blamed for his situation) do operate within some of the generalist health and welfare services that constitute the main avenues for professional help for male victims. Moreover, some of those gender-biases might have operated within the field in ways that have prevented the development of services for male victims or of family violence services that are designed to serve both male and female victims.

The issues for male victims seem, on the surface, to be very similar to those that operate for female victims, but the critical differences might be prevalence, level of fear and intimidation, and the degree to which male victims feel trapped in their circumstances in the same ways that female victims often are. The research that we have reported here should assist researchers in designing studies to effectively examine these difficult questions of prevalence and gender differences. Regardless of any gender differences in prevalence or severity, our findings indicate that it is important to provide specific services for male victims that are staffed by counsellors and other workers who are specifically trained in responding to male victims' needs. It is also important to conduct public education campaigns that raise the profile of male victims in ways that do not discount public understanding of violence against women and children. One way of doing this is to have public awareness and education programmes that deal with issues of family violence generally and include research-based information about male victims and female perpetrators.

6.3 Recommendations

On the basis of our findings in this research we make four key recommendations.

These recommendations are broad rather than specific because our data are exploratory and our research aimed to raise questions and guide future research rather than to answer the big questions about prevalence and level of service need. Much more research is needed on the topic of male victims of IPA. Nonetheless, male victims clearly exist and a strong theme in our data is male victims' fears about being believed, taken seriously and provided with effective support and assistance (including ensuring their safety). No doubt there are men who falsely claim to be victims (some of whom might in fact be perpetrators) just as some women make false allegations. However, much research with victims of all kinds (family violence, sexual assault, robbery, common assault, corruption, workplace or schoolyard harassment and bullying, etc.) and of both sexes tells us that a sceptical response to all reports by those whose role is to support and assist victims leads not only to further abuse of genuine victims but to lower levels of reporting such crimes and civil wrongs. Indeed our own data in Stage One of this research indicates that a fear of such scepticism at either a societal level or from an individual service provider is a major factor that prevents (or at least delays) men from disclosing abuse.

Our recommendations are:

1. That government funded public awareness campaigns be conducted to raise awareness of intimate partner violence against men. Such campaigns need to be very carefully designed so as to complement campaigns about family violence against women and children and not to damage the effectiveness of those campaigns.

2. Consideration should be given to providing publically-funded services specifically for male victims of IPA.

3. Consideration should be given to how services for male victims of IPA can be integrated with services for female victims and general services for victims of family violence in all its forms. It is likely that some types of service can be effectively integrated while others will need to be gender-specific.

4. Workers in the broader health and welfare fields should be provided with training to assist them to respond effectively to male victims of IPA. In particular, these workers need training in how to dismantle the barriers (identified in our research) to men disclosing their abuse and strengthening the factors that facilitate men's disclosure of their abuse.

I have separated the paragraphs of the recommendations and rendered them in bold type to illustrate exactly what sensible recommendations look like. These sensible recommendations were made **nine years ago**, around the time the Labor Government produced its twelve year *'National Plan to Reduce Violence against Women and their Children 2010-2022'*. Note there is no mention of men in Labor's national plan. The title could have read, 'National Plan to Reduce Domestic Violence 2010-2022', and have funding handed out with an even hand to address all types of domestic violence but as previously discussed, there were reasons this didn't happen.

BEING DOUBLY ABUSED

We all hear about discrimination and how there are laws against it. Speech is not as free as it once was and many factions of society are protected by anti discrimination laws but did you know that the Government continually discriminates all the time?

Think about it. Different rates of assistance for different groups of people when, if there was no discrimination, everyone should receive the same amounts. The aforementioned *'National Plan to Reduce Violence against Women and their Children 2010-2022,'* no mention of men here. If you look around there is evidence of discrimination all through Government attitudes and approaches to various factions in society. How does this come about? I have explored this question and the answer I received when I was discriminated against by a Government Department was that the discrimination was legislated for. In other words, although there is an anti discrimination law, it is modified by other laws which can override it and allow discrimination by the Australian Government.

As an example, here are some excerpts from the Sex Discrimination Act 1984 amended to Dec 2018.

Part 1 Preliminary.

5 Sex discrimination

(1) For the purposes of this Act, a person (in this subsection referred to as the ***discriminator***) discriminates against another person (in this subsection referred to as the ***aggrieved***

person) on the ground of the sex of the aggrieved person if, by reason of:

(a) the sex of the aggrieved person;

(b) a characteristic that appertains generally to persons of the sex of the aggrieved person; or

(c) a characteristic that is generally imputed to persons of the sex of the aggrieved person;

the discriminator treats the aggrieved person less favourably than, in circumstances that are the same or are not materially different, the discriminator treats or would treat a person of a different sex.

(2) For the purposes of this Act, a person (the *discriminator*) discriminates against another person (the *aggrieved person*) on the ground of the sex of the aggrieved person if the discriminator imposes, or proposes to impose, a condition, requirement or practice that has, or is likely to have, the effect of disadvantaging persons of the same sex as the aggrieved person.

6 Discrimination on the ground of marital or relationship status

(1) For the purposes of this Act, a person (in this subsection referred to as the *discriminator*) discriminates against another person (in this subsection referred to as the *aggrieved person*) on the ground of the marital or relationship status of the aggrieved person if, by reason of:

(a) the marital or relationship status of the aggrieved person; or

(b) a characteristic that appertains generally to persons of the marital or relationship status of the aggrieved person; or

   (c) a characteristic that is generally imputed to persons of the marital or relationship status of the aggrieved person;

the discriminator treats the aggrieved person less favourably than, in circumstances that are the same or are not materially different, the discriminator treats or would treat a person of a different marital or relationship status.

   (2) For the purposes of this Act, a person (the *discriminator*) discriminates against another person (the *aggrieved person*) on the ground of the marital or relationship status of the aggrieved person if the discriminator imposes, or proposes to impose, a condition, requirement or practice that has, or is likely to have, the effect of disadvantaging persons of the same marital or relationship status as the aggrieved person.

Division 2 – Discrimination in other areas

26 Administration of Commonwealth laws and programs

   (1) It is unlawful for a person who performs any function or exercises any power under a Commonwealth law or for the purposes of a Commonwealth program, or has any other responsibility for the administration of a Commonwealth law or the conduct of a Commonwealth program, to discriminate against another person, on the ground of the other person's sex, sexual orientation, gender identity, intersex status, marital or relationship status, pregnancy or potential pregnancy, or breastfeeding, in the performance of that function, the exercise of that power or the fulfilment of that responsibility.

   (2) This section binds the Crown in right of a State.

From the above one would assume that in terms of assistance for victims of domestic violence, whether men or women, it would be provided on equal grounds regardless of the sex of the applicant. However, it is obvious that this is not so in practice and it's very apparent that abused men are openly discriminated against by their own Government when seeking assistance. How so? Read on.

Division 4 -- Exemptions

32 Services for members of one sex

Nothing in Division 1 or 2 applies to or in relation to the provision of services the nature of which is such that they can only be provided to members of one sex.

40 Acts done under statutory authority

(2) Nothing in Division 1 or 2 affects anything done by a person in direct compliance with any of the following as in force on 1 August 1984:

(a) the *Gift Duty Assessment Act 1941*;

(b) the operation of:

(i) the definition of *pensioner* in subsection 4(1); or

(ii) the definition of *concessional beneficiary* in subsection 84(1);

of the *National Health Act 1953*;

(c) the *Income Tax Assessment Act 1936*;

(d) the *International Tax Agreements Act 1953*;

(e) the *Papua New Guinea (Members of the Forces Benefits) Act 1957*;

(f) the *Sales Tax (Exemptions and Classifications) Act 1935*;

(h) the *Social Security Act 1947*;

(i) the *Taxation (Unpaid Company Tax) Assessment Act 1982*;

(j) the *Social Services Act 1980* of Norfolk Island.

Besides the rider in the anti discrimination legislation regarding services for one sex (read women only) the Social Security Act 1947 is just one of the many Acts which allows the Government to circumvent the Anti Discrimination legislation and provide services solely to women. Services which are generally unavailable to men or the requirements for those services are set at such a high level for men that they are unlikely to be realised.

Why has this come about?

Domestic violence is composed of many factors. As has been seen from various scientific articles, these factors are being classified and reclassified constantly to achieve some sort of agreement on what actually constitutes domestic violence. Throughout all of these adjustments, verbal abuse remains one of the leading contenders in the domestic violence pantheon. As we have seen from the Australian Governments own report – Family, Domestic and Sexual Violence in Australia 2018 plus many other studies over the years, many of which appear above, emotional and verbal domestic abuse is split nearly fifty percent between partners depending on which figures are used. The problem for men is that they are usually physically larger than women and have the ability to inflict more damage to their partner if the violence escalates, than their partner can inflict on them. The result of this is women who bear the obvious results of conflict and appear in A&E for treatment. There are however, many previously discussed reasons why men don't appear for treatment at A&E as statistically often as they could or should.

I can almost feel the surge of denial from the feminist front as I write this and I have no intention of belittling those women who have suffered from years of abuse at the hands of their partners, it is well documented and I feel sorry for them but this book isn't about the women who suffer from domestic violence, there are reams written about them, its about the men. Less well documented however, are the men who have suffered years of abuse at the hands of their partners and who have no recourse to assistance.

The end result of women being more seriously injured than men in cases of domestic conflict and appearing for medical assistance more often has helped result in domestic violence being classified as a 'Gendered Crime'. In other words, domestic violence is a crime perpetrated by men only. In spite of much research being done by many organisations both in Australia and overseas which show that this may not necessarily be the case, the Australian Government has adopted this viewpoint. It is not alone in doing so. The result of this is:-

National Plan to Reduce Violence Against Women and their Children 2010-2022

(The National Plan) identifies DFV and sexual assault as **gendered**

crimes that have an unequal impact on women and as the most pervasive forms of violence experienced by women in Australia (Council of Australian Governments, 2011). Three-quarters (17.3% or 1,625,000) of victim-survivors of intimate partner violence in Australia are women, compared to men who account for one-quarter of victim-survivors (6.1% or 547,600) (ABS, 2017).

The use of the term 'gendered crime', in spite of over one quarter of the victim survivors being *male* (see above) has enabled the production of a national plan to reduce violence against women and provide support by means of 'safe' houses, accommodation and many other forms of assistance which male victims of domestic violence cannot access. This is discrimination on a vast scale – 547,600 *male* victim survivors in 2017 – only those that were reported, unable to receive support due to being discriminated against because they are male. Where is the equality in that? Are all men now victims of the labels which are being attached to gender? Granted, the number of female victims is three times that of male victims but there were still over half a million affected men who could not access a system which has been set up solely for female victims. I personally know the frustration and sense of helplessness when no one wants to help because you are a male victim of domestic violence and the system is not designed to help you.

Why not?

So, as a man you want to claim discrimination against you on the basis of gender? Good luck. The Government has neatly exempted itself from this claim by listing the exemptions reproduced in the Acts above. Somewhere in the Exemptions to the Anti Discrimination Act will be the means for the Government to exclude over half a million of the citizens it is supposed to serve, from accessing basic humanitarian assistance. You have not only been abused by your partner, your Government has abused you again by turning its back on you in your time of need. Legally.

However, it gets worse. Men who ring *some* support lines in Victoria and NSW because they are actual victims of physical abuse from their female partners are being referred through to telephone counselling designed for male perpetrators of domestic violence because *everyone knows that only men commit domestic violence.* So they must be the one at fault.

Now there is a move afoot to have every woman presenting at A&E with some form of injury to be asked if their partner caused the injury. Note, not every *person* presenting at A&E but only every women. Remember that 25% figure for male victim survivors of domestic violence. This move once again underlines the blatant sexual discrimination in domestic violence cases and what is more interesting is that female on male physical domestic violence is increasing. Will men at A&E be asked if their injuries were spouse related? I doubt it.

THE DOUBLE STANDARD

Once again risking the ire of the more strident of the feminist movement, I will start this chapter with an example of the court of public opinion.

A little while ago in Australia, a news item broke regarding a young man who had committed domestic violence while he was gaming online. It was visually recorded in a corner of the screen and provoked outrage by all and sundry, garnering a top spot on the ABC seven o'clock news with the recording of his 'violence' being broadcast. The court of public opinion had him hung drawn and quartered for his 'offence'. But what did we see? A young man gaming (he had been for six hours apparently). A young woman enters the room and demands he stop and do something she wants him to do. He replies that he wants to continue with his game and asks to be left alone. She returns and when he doesn't comply with her demands, throws a *flattened* cardboard box at him, the corner of which hits him in the head. He gets up and goes off camera and we hear squeals and grunts. Guilty.

Let's turn this around. A young woman has been sewing a dress for six hours and is intent on finishing it. A young man enters and demands she leave what she is doing to do something he wants her to do. She tells him to leave her alone as she wants to finish the dress. He returns and makes demands again culminating in throwing a flattened cardboard box at her, the edge of which hits her in the head. She gets up and retaliates. Once again he's the one guilty of initiating domestic violence and she is quite justified in retaliating. This case has recently resulted in a conviction for the young man even though it was reported he had 'objects' thrown at him by the young woman *before* he retaliated. Does this outcome give tacit approval for women to throw things at their partners in a domestic scenario without legal repercussion?

Another example is a research exercise in perceived public opinion which has been doing the rounds on Facebook and Youtube. In this video, shot in a public place, we see actors, a man and woman start a fight and begin a shouting match before the man is seen to 'hit' the woman. Bystanders register shock and onlookers rush in to assist the 'victim'. In the next scene the initial conditions are re-enacted, only this time the woman is seen to hit the man. Bystanders are seen to laugh and point, seemingly amused by the conflict but no one comes to the man's aid.

In both of the above scenarios we see the application of double standards. From where does this arise? Let us return to the hunter gatherer forebears for part of the answer. The book, 'The Selfish Gene' by Richard Dawkins proposes that our entire existence is directed to passing on our genetic component into the future. In the case of men it means protecting the woman who nurtures the child you made together. By protecting and feeding her as she cares for the child, you are in effect protecting your genetic heritage. This is an evolutionary trait which still exists in present day society, although it seems to be weakening (my opinion). This protective urge translated into the code of chivalry after the Dark Ages and in many areas of society women were treated with great deference which culminated in the Romanticism of the Victorian era. From that time on, women have shaken off their shackles in a bid to become equal to men. As previously noted, equal does not necessarily mean 'the same as'. However, there is still that genetic imperative in force and women are still protected, even when they use violence. This is not new. We all know the little women can't hurt us. But she can and does. Around the beginning of the nineteen hundreds it became popular for women to administer rat poison (arsenic) to husbands they wanted rid of. There are many accounts of this regarding women who were actually caught but the true figure will never be known, as only those apprehended contribute to the official figures. Many a man may have wasted away or taken ill and died without it being noted as murder because post mortems were not so common in those days.

Since the era of silent movies we have seen men getting their faces slapped for some transgression or other. It was a part of growing up for a lot of people – this acceptance of women hitting men. In the days of manners and chivalry it was a way for women to stop an unwanted advance in its tracks. Society has since evolved with the idea that it is okay for women to hit men in this way, what harm could they do? Unfortunately this once simple act has evolved and morphed into an ingrained double standard which still seems to be acceptable to both women and some men. Because of this double standard, women's violence is being downplayed and its effects are being minimalized in all corners of society.

Combine this double standard with the vastly increased consumption of alcohol by today's younger women and the concurrent lessening of inhibitions and permissions assumed from social media. We have increased trigger events in relationships resulting in someone getting hurt and usually, the man getting the blame.

Another insidious side effect of this unconscious genetic urge to protect women are the results of court cases involving female violence. I personally know someone whose friend was set free after murdering her husband by *claiming* years of domestic violence. It is a popular defence by women who murder their spouses and those cases where women win their freedom would not enter the statistics for men murdered by their spouse, as no conviction would be recorded. I have on my desk an article from the local paper concerning three separate cases involving women and domestic violence. In two cases no conviction was recorded, even though one of these charges involved obstructing police. This scenario is being played out right across the country and as many statistics used in domestic violence reports are calculated from actual convictions, we can see where some of the bias in those statistics and figures can occur.

For men, the story is the opposite. It seems that in the present climate men have to be made an example of and often suffer at the hands of the judiciary. In a situation where blows have been exchanged between the man and woman in a relationship, it is most often the man who is charged with assault and suffers the consequences. These consequences affect his right to see his children and often result in an AVO being granted to the woman, effectively blocking the man from the family home which he still has to pay for.

As previously discussed, with research to back up the figures, we are seeing more and more examples of the increase in the numbers and percentage of women who use physical violence in their relationships. What we are not seeing is a concomitant realisation of this by those involved in assisting the victims of domestic violence, both women *and* men. Help is currently not distributed on a needs basis, it is distributed on the basis of gender and the sooner this can be rectified, the better.

As an example of this bias, I have reproduced most of the wording from the cover of a document released by a national organization solely dealing with *women's* safety.

ANROWS is a research organisation for women's safety, producing risk assessment for the Commonwealth Department of Social Services. How much emphasis is placed on male victims of domestic violence and their risks? A brief perusal of the document revealed virtually no mention of male victims. Once again we see double standards being applied.

National Risk Assessment Principles: Companion resource for the Commonwealth Department of Social Services.

National Risk Assessment Principles for domestic and family violence:

Companion resource

A summary of the evidence-base supporting the development and implementation of the National Risk Assessment Principles for domestic and family violence.

CORINA BACKHOUSE AND CHERIE TOIVONEN

Australia's National Research Organisation for Women's Safety, for the Commonwealth Department of Social Services

ANROWS - to reduce violence against women and their children

This document is titled as a companion resource for domestic and family violence and is purported to be a summary of an *evidence-base* to support the development and implementation of the National Risk Assessment Principles for domestic and family violence. With that title one would expect no gender bias but ANROWS is itself gender biased as it deals solely with women's safety. It is also a resource for the Commonwealth Department of Social Services.

To recap. More than one quarter (25%) of victim survivors of domestic violence are male and over one fifth (20%) of domestic violence deaths are men at the hands of women yet there is an ongoing continual bias and discrimination against providing aid to male victims. Why. They hurt too and suicide often. There is a double standard at work here. Most of the politicians involved in a lot of the legislature surrounding domestic violence are sensitive to the fact that around half of their voting public are female and many of those politicians are old school, no doubt having a chivalrous attitude towards protecting women. There is nothing wrong with that but in taking such a stance and declaring domestic violence to be solely *gender based* has excluded around 25% of its victims. It's time for the legislation to be changed to allow all victims to access help in their time of need.

HOW AND WHERE TO GET HELP

How does this double standard affect the ability of men to access emergency shelter for themselves and their children if they are one of the 25% of domestic violence victims who are suffering violence at the hands of their female spouse?

The answer is not good. The Government has provided millions of dollars of funding to set up safe housing for women. This is handled by the States not the Federal Government so there will be differences in outcomes depending on which State of Australia you live in, as different States seem to have differing opinions on who is responsible for domestic violence. However, the Australian Government does fund some national help lines. It appears that some of these Helplines are mostly for counselling rather than immediate help. However, once they've talked with you, a councillor can direct you to the relative State agency which *may* then provide assistance. Some useful contacts are listed below but there are other organisations which can help you, take some time to look them up.

If you are feeling really bad and thoughts of self harm/suicide are passing through your mind, call the following immediately.

Lifeline 13 11 14 If you are on the edge and you need to talk to someone, give them a call immediately. These people are highly trained and motivated to help you. It just might save your life.

1800Respect (1800 737 732) is a National sexual assault, domestic family violence counselling service who can talk or chat with you and offer referrals to the relative agencies. I found them helpful and honest when talking about domestic violence against men. However, when I used the website I found no matching results for crisis accommodation or shelter and housing in Queensland.

MensLine Australia 1300 78 99 78 or go to mensline.org.au It is funded by the Australian Government Department of Social Services and is delivered by On the Line. This organisation runs a website on which, after a bit of digging around, I found the following article which is very useful for men. It also illustrates that the Australian Government Department of Social Services is aware of the problem facing many men with regard to being victims of domestic violence but doesn't act to deal with them in the same manner as it deals with women who are facing similar circumstances.

Mensline Australia Tip Sheet

Are you experiencing violence or abuse in your relationship?

Men also experience family and domestic violence.

Violence and abuse can take many forms but the most common include physical violence and threats, emotional abuse, social and financial control, and persistent demeaning comments.

Violence and abuse in intimate relationships includes:

• Physical assault – slapping, hitting, scratching

• Emotional and psychological abuse –belittling remarks, yelling, screaming, put-downs, being ignored, constant criticism

• *Limited decision making – having all decisions relating to finances, purchases, lifestyle and living arrangements made for you*

• *Social isolation – being unreasonably restricted from your family or friends*

• *Dominating behaviour – behaviour designed to deliberately frighten, harm or control you*

(i.e. threatening to harm you, themselves or someone else).

No one person's experience is typical. Violence and abuse in intimate relationships have many different combinations of controlling behaviour and can also change over time.

Questions to ask yourself

• *Do you feel safe in your current relationship?*

• *Are you insulted, demeaned or criticised in public by your partner?*

• *Is living with your partner like 'walking on eggshells'?*

• *Does your partner prevent you from doing things that are important to you? E.g. seeing family or friends*

• *Does your partner threaten you?*

• *Do you feel like you are in an abusive relationship?*

• *Are your partner's needs the only ones allowed to be met in the relationship?*

Impact of violence and abuse

Experiencing violence and abuse, even over a short time, can lead to long-standing changes in a person, including:

• *Feelings of helplessness, depression, worthlessness, powerlessness and isolation*

• *Feelings of shame, guilt and despair*

• *Chronic health problems (including psychological problems), physical injury and*

shortened lifespan

• *Difficulty in functioning in other parts of your life – in particular at work, but also among your social group.*

Will I be believed?

There is now far greater understanding of the frequency of men as victims of violence and abuse in their intimate relationships. It is important to remember:

• *Men, like everyone, are entitled to the full protection of the law*

• *If you are at risk of injury, it is better to report it to the police than do nothing or act out physically*

• *You are entitled to be treated with respect.*

If you are not satisfied appropriate action is being taken to protect you, report it again until your situation is understood and your safety is being addressed.

What can I do?

Report it

Let someone else know what is going on. Talk with a person in a position of authority (police, lawyer, doctor) who will know your rights and responsibilities or who can put you in contact with a professional for expert advice. When contacting police, in some circumstances they will be required to take action if your safety is at risk.

Get support

It is important that you find someone you can confide in about your situation. Talking about what is happening is very important and can undo some of the feelings of isolation and helplessness that are common in men who are the victims of violence and abuse. This person can have specialist skills such as counselling, but that is not essential; it needs to be someone who will listen to you carefully and be available as you move through the process of working out how to manage the situation.

Call MensLine Australia on 1300 78 99 78 for support and to discuss your options.

Develop a safety plan

Develop a safety plan if you believe your safety, or the safety of others, could be at risk. The safety plan is a predetermined course of action to use when you decide there is an imminent risk of violence or psychological harm (children can be harmed psychologically when witnessing repeated abuse).

The safety plan is designed to create distance and remove the likelihood of an incident happening, and may include things such as:

• Under what circumstances will you leave the family home? Where will you go that is safe?

What is your long-term plan?

• *Will you take the children with you? Do you have the right to take the children with you?*

• *Who needs to know that you have activated your safety plan?*

Keep a journal of incidents. This could be useful if you need legal protection or police intervention.

Will your partner change?

A change in your partner's behaviour is unlikely to occur without them obtaining professional assistance. Your partner may feel remorse after an abusive incident, but the abuse is unlikely to stop unless they seek help or you remove yourself from the situation.

The decision to stay or leave a relationship is yours alone. However, talk through your decision with trusted others beforehand. Understand what you lose or gain from staying in a relationship, or from leaving.

MensLine Australia is available 24 hours a day, seven days a week, with professional counsellors providing information and support for all relationship issues. Call us on 1300 78 99 78 or visit mensline.org.au.

This is very sensible advice and gives me some hope in the ability of the Australian Government Dept. of Social Services to start addressing the problem of male victims of domestic violence in a more proactive manner and to help men in times of need. Note the advice about keeping a journal or diary of incidents, you will need to prove your case. Also, although it is inadmissible in court, some people have been known to voice record an incident. Today's mobile phones make this easy and discreet. If the police then become involved in the situation there is some form of record of the conflict.

DV Connect Mensline 1800 811 811 Private organisation funded by Qld Gov.

I rang them and discovered that this is primarily a counselling service. The person I spoke to was very pleasant and helpful. When I asked about safe houses or emergency accommodation I was given the number for the Homeless Hotline. I rang to discuss emergency accommodation for men suffering from ongoing domestic violence only to be reminded that if they were not homeless there was nowhere for them to be placed. Apparently there is a gap in Queensland for safe accommodation, if needed, for the 25% of domestic violence sufferers who just happen to be male.

Police 000 Remember that the police are there to help and in most situations will assist in dealing with a violent woman. Don't stay in the house if you are being physically attacked, get out and stay out until the police arrive. If the woman follows you out of the house to continue the violence, make yourself scarce until the police turn up. What will happen then and in the future, depends entirely on the responding police officers. Your future is in their hands.

Men's Referral Service 1300 766 491 supported by the Victorian Gov, the Tasmanian Gov and the NSW Gov-Women NSW

My perusal of this website indicates it is set up for men who commit domestic violence or are thinking of it. I could find no reference to men as victims of domestic violence or any indication that such people actually exist. When I rang, I was told that the purpose of the site was to council men who were perpetrators of domestic violence. When I asked about assisting men who were victims, I was given the number of Victims Services. When I rang them I was told they don't have emergency housing for male victims of domestic violence.

Personally, I would *not* ring this site if I was a male *victim* of domestic violence. The last thing you need to be told when you're being hurt and injured is that you are the one responsible for the violence being committed against you.

Black Ribbon Foundation has a Facebook page but I couldn't find a phone number. It was set up to help men who are having trouble with domestic violence in their relationship. I left a message which wasn't answered and you have to log into Facebook to get the page open.

This is not an exhaustive list of contacts. There will be many more than this but these are the main ones. If you suspect that you may require help in the future, try to look up some local services in your area before you need to use them.

THE LAST WORD

If you are a man reading this, who is the partner of a violent woman, you have my sympathy. It's difficult to know what to do. In my experience I found I should have left the relationship long before I did and accepted the consequences of my actions at the time. Staying on was a trial I did not need in my life, even if it did forge me in the flames.

We never set out to make a 'bad' decision and at the time of making a decision we always try to make the best one we can make with the information we have at hand. It is only with the benefit of hindsight do we realise some of our decisions could have been much better. It's exactly the same making decisions in a relationship. Never retaliate against violence unless it's to save your own life, just leave the scene. Quickly if necessary. After my marriage ended I subsequently heard my ex wife had pursued a boyfriend down the street to punch him in the head. Nothing will be gained by satisfying the desire to 'get one back', 'dominate', 'satisfy a bruised ego' or 'take control'. That way leads to a world of woes and sometimes very serious repercussions. Take control of your own ego and walk away, or run if you have to, things will eventually work out.

However dark life seems, there is always a helping hand somewhere. Swallow your pride and realise you are not alone. Call for help and talk to a sympathetic listener, be it a professional or a friend. Report your position to authorities if necessary. Suicide never solves anything. Take a deep breath, hold your head up and carry on with your life, yet another survivor of female domestic violence. There are quite a lot of us out here, mostly living a 'normal' life, which is what you can do once you free yourself from a damaging woman.

If you are reading this and are part of the Government or any organisation which deals with domestic violence, take note of the evidence presented and do something to help the 25% of domestic violence sufferers who are male. It's not a joke. Forget the mantra, 'Only men commit domestic violence', all the evidence, both scientific and anecdotal shows otherwise. Those 546,000 men bashed by their women in 2017 needed help. Not ten years in the future -- NOW!

If you are a woman reading this. Sexual discrimination is abhorrent to women but in regards to this situation, many women seem quite happy to have it happen to men. Fairness, often proclaimed but not so often put into place, is what this issue is about. Sometimes, to be equal, there needs to be giving. Men who are victims of domestic violence perpetrated by women should have the same rights and access to resources as female victims of domestic violence. The bottom line is they don't and male suicides caused by this predicament far outstrips that of women. This issue needs to be publicised.

NOW

Made in the USA
Middletown, DE
16 January 2023

21606200R00060